People
of the
Covenant

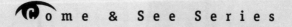

Come & See Series

The **Come & See Series** from Sheed & Ward is
modeled on Jesus' compassionate question: "What
do you seek?" and his profound invitation to
"Come and see" the world through the eyes of
faith (John 1:38–39). The series offers spiritual
seekers lively, thought-provoking, and accessible
books that explore topics of faith and the Catholic
Christian tradition. Each book in the series is written
by trustworthy guides who are the very best teachers,
theologians, and scholars.

Series Editors: James Martin, S.J.
Jeremy Langford

People
of the
Covenant

An
Invitation
to the
Old Testament

Dianne Bergant, CSA

SHEED & WARD
Franklin, Wisconsin

As an apostolate of the Priests of the Sacred Heart, a Catholic religious congregation, the mission of Sheed & Ward is to publish books of contemporary impact and enduring merit in Catholic Christian thought and action. The books published, however, reflect the opinions of their authors and are not meant to represent the official position of the Priests of the Sacred Heart.

2001

Sheed & Ward
7373 South Lovers Lane Road
Franklin, Wisconsin 53132
1-800-266-5564

Printed in the United States of America

Cover and interior design: Biner Design and GrafixStudio, Inc.

Cover art: "Peasants of the Middle East"

Scripture quotations are from the New Revised Standard Version of the Bible, copyright 1989 by the Division of Christian Education of the National Council of the Churches of Christ in the USA. Used by permission. All rights reserved.

Library of Congress Cataloging-in-Publication Data

Bergant, Dianne.
    People of the covenant : an invitation to the Old Testament / Dianne
    Bergant
        p. cm. — (Come & see series)
    Includes bibliographical references and index.
    ISBN 1-58051-090-6 (alk. paper)
        1. Bible. O.T.—Biography. I. Title. II. Series.
BS571 .B47 2001
221.6'1—dc21
                                            00-054732
                                            CIP

1 2 3 4 5 / 04 03 02 01

Contents

Chapter 4 The Kings **/ 59**

Chapter 5 The Prophets **/ 75**

Chapter 6 The Priests **/ 97**

Chapter 7 The Wise Ones **/ 113**

Preface

The Christian Bible consists of two testaments or collections of writings. The First Testament, traditionally known as the Old Testament, comes from the people of ancient Israel and testifies to their faith in God. There are two generally accepted versions of this collection. The Protestant Bible, which follows the Jewish version, has thirty-nine books in its collection. The Roman Catholic Bible, which is the one used in this study, adopted the Greek collection and has forty-five books. (The translation used here is the New Revised Standard Version.) The history of this difference in the number of books in the collections, though quite interesting in itself, need not concern us here. The Second Testament, known as the New Testament, is the same for all Christian denominations. It contains twenty-seven books, all of which focus on Jesus and his significance in the lives of believers.

This book is a beginner's guide to the First Testament. Written as a companion to another volume in Sheed & Ward's Come and See Series entitled *Who Is Jesus? Why Is He Important? An Invitation to the New Testament*, by Daniel J. Harrington, S.J., *People of the Covenant* introduces readers to some of the most important teachings found in the First Testament by explaining the significance of certain people who appear in the pages of various biblical books. Using these people as a lens and organizing principle shows how faith in God developed and how it was expressed in ancient Israel down through the ages. It is important to remember that this teaching is preserved in various forms of expression, forms that must be accurately perceived if the message that they contain is to be understood. A short explanation of these forms is in order here.

The two major categories of literary expression are poetry and prose. We all know that these two types of literature are neither written nor understood in the same way. Poetry uses figurative language and forms of speech. It frequently describes what something is like rather than what it really is ("Your eyes are doves," Cant 1:15), and it expresses the emotions that the person or object generates ("Let the hearts of those who seek the LORD rejoice," Ps 105:3). On the other hand, prose is much more straightforward in its expression. Among other things, it relates events ("The priests bearing the ark of the covenant went in front of the people," Josh 3:14); it describes people ("He [Goliath] had a helmet of bronze on his head, and he was armed with a coat of mail," 1 Sam 17:5); and it states laws ("Observe the sabbath day," Deut 5:12). We will miss the point of the passage if we read prose as if it were poetry or poetry as if it were prose.

Finally, unlike the writings of the Second Testament, which were composed between the middle of the first century and the early years of the second century C.E. (Common Era) or A.D. (*anno Domini*, or Year of the Lord), the writings of the First Testament span a period of thousands of years, originate out of several historical periods and political situations, and address many different social or religious issues. All of this must be taken into consideration when we read the Bible. We must remember that the various biblical authors did not have us in mind when they wrote. Rather, they wrote for their own time. However, people of faith believed that to be faithful to the religious traditions that they inherited from their ancestors, they would have to interpret these traditions in ways that would be meaningful to a new generation. As we enter into the twenty-first century, this challenge to understand in new ways faces us as well. Although this guide will present some of the contents of the First Testament, it will do so with an eye to this challenge of interpretation.

Chapter 1

An Introduction

There are basically three ways of studying the Bible. The first and foremost way is as a piece of literature. More especially, the Bible is a compendium of pieces of literature. As ancient Near Eastern writing, it utilizes the literary forms, techniques, and imagery of the ancient world. As with all writing, we must understand its literary character if we are to grasp its meaning. Finally, much of the biblical material was originally oral in form, handed down from generation to generation by word of mouth. As it was handed down, cultural reshaping took place. What we have is the fruit of constant adding, subtracting, editing, and reediting.

Second, the Bible is a book of theology. This means that the primary purpose of its many and varied writings was not simple reporting, whether such reporting be historical, scientific, or psychological. Rather, over the generations, the writers intended to provide religious interpretation of the events of their lives. The complexity of the transmission of these religious traditions, as mentioned above, resulted in a variety of theological writings, some of which appear at first glance to contradict others. We must remember that the writings are religious reflections on aspects of life, and these aspects were influenced by the constant change of circumstances.

Finally, the very character of the writings tells us something about the social, political, economic, and cultural history of the ancient Israelite people. Although it is not a book of history as we have come to understand that type of writing, it leads us through many of the historical events of Israel's life.

It is impossible to study the Bible exclusively from one of these three points of view. Any section from any book reveals aspects of all three approaches. However, books about the Bible generally select one way as the primary approach. The reader of this book will see that some sections concentrate on literary aspects, while other sections are more concerned with the theological or the historical. This all attests to the richness of the Bible's compostions.

The First Testament Itself

The foreword to the Book of Sirach identifies the three headings under which the books of the First Testament have been listed: the Law, the Prophets, and the Writings. This division is influenced by literary categories. The Law is more than legal statements. Also known by its Greek name, Pentateuch (five books), it is really the extensive *narrative* found in the first five books of the Bible. Although the section called the Prophets includes stories about the prophets, it is primarily the collection of their teachings known as *prophecies*. The Writings include: *short stories* like Ruth, Esther, Judith, and Tobit; *poetry* like the Psalms, Lamentations, Proverbs, Job, Qoheleth, the Song of Songs, Sirach, and the Wisdom of Solomon. While there is general agreement regarding the order of books, in some places the Roman Catholic Bible is arranged in a slightly different fashion, one that gives the impression of the unfolding of a historical narrative.

Biblical authorship is a rather complex issue. While the material certainly comes from human beings, people of faith believe that these traditions are inspired by God. This means that they possess divine authorship and, for this reason, they are referred to as the *word of God*. Sometimes the books are named for events described within them (Genesis, Exodus), for people about whom the stories are written (Samuel, Judith), or for the kind of material found there (Psalms, Proverbs). At other times they bear the names of the prophets whose teachings are collected therein (Isaiah, Jeremiah). Even in those books, authorship can mean various things. For example, there is no doubt that much of the teaching in the Book of Isaiah came from that prophet (Isaiah 1–39). However, later disciples of Isaiah, writing in the tradition of his thought, added material to this collection and attributed it to the original prophet (Isaiah 40–55; 56–66).

There is still another kind of authorship that has less to do with the actual writing than with the authority behind it. In this vane, Moses is credited for the writing of the first five books of the Bible—Genesis, Exodus, Leviticus, Numbers, and Deuteronomy. It is unlikely that he actually wrote any of them, particularly the account of his own death! However, because of his importance as a spokesperson of God, attributing his name to those traditions gave them a share in his authority. The same is true with respect to the Psalms that are attributed to David and the wisdom books that are assigned to Solomon.

The earliest version of the Bible was written in Hebrew. With the conquest of the world by Alexander the Great, the Greek language became the spoken language of most of the people. This meant that the sacred traditions of Israel were often foreign to the Greek-speaking Jews. Thus, the need of a Greek version became apparent. A popular legend recounts how seventy-two elders, six from each of the twelve tribes of Israel, working separately, produced identical translations. This miraculous outcome was considered evidence of the inspired nature of the translation, which is known as the Septuagint or LXX (seventy, the rounded number of the translators). As mentioned earlier, the Protestant First Testament comes from the Hebrew listing, while the Roman Catholic Bible follows the format of this Septuagint collection.

The World of Ancient Israel

The earliest political organization found in the biblical narratives was tribal. People who lived in close proximity or who were somehow related to one another were gathered together into tribes, which were named after a significant ancestor.

The most prominent names that have survived are Reuben, Simeon, Levi, Judah, Zebulun, Issachar, Dan, Gad, Ashur, Naphtali, Joseph, and Benjamin (see Gen 49:1–28). These men were said to be the sons of Jacob, who was the son of Isaac, who was the son of Abraham, the Father, or primary ancestor, of the Israelite people. The historical accuracy of this tradition is less important than its religious significance. It traces people from a much later period back to a promise believed to have been made by God to an ancestor, a promise of multiple descendants and prosperity in a land given to them by God (see Gen 15:5, 18).

Although the tribes were relatively independent of each other, they did hold many important things in common. For example, they believed that they were all descendants of the same ancestors who had been called by God; they considered themselves a special people committed to their God through a legal contract known as a *covenant*; they came together at regular intervals to worship and to celebrate their God's goodness to them; they were governed basically by the same laws that, they believed, had been delivered to them from their God at the time of their entrance into the covenant; they were obliged to assist each other militarily if the need ever arose. This loosely joined organization lasted for about two hundred years, circa 1200–1060 B.C.E., or Before Common Era. (Modern scholarship uses this more general designation rather than the religious expression "Before Christ.") During this time the tribes consolidated their own respective identities as well as their communal sense of themselves as the "people of God."

Tribal independence too frequently resulted in selfish indifference toward the well-being of other tribes. The major threat to the individual tribes was the Ammonite nation, a well-organized people who was able to divide and conquer. It became very clear to some in the tribal federation that the only way the people of God would survive this danger would be through the agency of a strong central power. This meant the establishment of a monarchy. In Israel, however, there was significant opposition to this shift in government and religious understanding. Not only were people unwilling to relinquish their power to a leader who was not of their tribe, but some of the more religiously minded believed that such a move would be a violation of their covenant with God, who was their true and only king. Ultimately a king was chosen, the people were united under his leadership, and a new phase of existence began.

The first king, Saul, was a rustic man, more a military leader than a political administrator. He was succeeded by David, who began as a military strategist and ended as a powerful political ruler. The peace and prosperity established by David, however, was short lived. Although his son Solomon succeeded him, with Solomon's death (922 B.C.E.) the nation split into two kingdoms, each with its own king (Israel in the north and Judah in the south). This situation prevailed for about two hundred years, until the northern kingdom of Israel was overrun by the Assyrians (722 B.C.E.) The southern kingdom of Judah was spared this onslaught and continued to be ruled by a descendant of David until the Babylonians moved on it, defeated its military forces, destroyed Jerusalem, its capitol, and took many of its leading citizens into exile in Babylon (587 B.C.E.).

The kingdom of David was destroyed, never to be resurrected with the same glory and significance that it had once known. In fact, the nation would be a colony first of the Persians (538 B.C.E.), then of the Greeks (333 B.C.E.), and finally of the Romans (63 B.C.E.). Only during the brief time of the Maccabees (166–63 B.C.E.) did the nation enjoy any kind of independence. Around 70 C.E. the people were finally defeated by their Roman occupiers and dispersed across the face of the earth. This condition of being a people without political identity lasted until 1948, when the modern state of Israel was born.

During each period of Israel's history, the people always clung to the belief that they were God's chosen people, but the circumstances of their existence influenced how they understood this belief. Peace and prosperity were seen as rewards for fidelity to their covenant commitment; misfortune was considered punishment from God for violation of their sacred pact. This is a clear example of how religious understanding develops out of the experience of life, interprets that experience, and directs future experience.

The God of Israel

The earliest traditions of ancient Israel speak of God as the one who, "with a strong hand and an outstretched arm" (Deut 26:8), delivered the people from bondage. This was the God who had spoken to Moses from a bush that burned but was not consumed (see Exod 3:2); the God who, in the land of Egypt itself, demanded that the pharaoh "let my people go!" (see Exod 3:10); the God who led the people dry-shod through the sea (see Exodus 14:29) and fed them in the wilderness (see Exod 16:13–21); the God who strengthened them in battle as they entered the land that had been promised to them (see Josh 1:11). God clearly was their deliverer, their savior.

When David occupied the Jebusite city of Jerusalem and set up his own rule there, he seems merely to have taken over the organization established by the people he had conquered. The defeat of one people by another always meant that the god of the victors was more powerful than the god of the vanquished. For example, there is evidence that the early inhabitants of Jerusalem worshiped a creator-god called God Most High (see Gen 14:18–20), but David's conquest indicated that his God was really the Most High God. It was probably from that time on that the God of Israel was thought of as creator as well as deliverer.

Throughout Israel's history, various other images were used to speak about God. These images all arose out of the people's experience. The intimate bond of the covenant was often compared to a marriage, and God was portrayed as a faithful husband (see Isaiah 54:4). In describing the steadfastness of divine love, God was depicted as a woman who would never forget the child at her breast (see Isa 49:15). God was also described as an eagle that both protectively hovered over its brood and bore it aloft on its pinions (see Deut 32:11). Finally, God was frequently characterized as a sturdy rock upon which one could depend (see Pss 28:1; 42:9; 62:2, 6, 7; 78:35; 89:26; 94:22).

God was known by many names. The most common was the simple designation "God." In early times this title was qualified in various ways. God was identified with the ancestors: the God of Abraham (see Gen 31:42) or the Shield of Abram (see Gen 15:1); the God of Isaac (see Gen 32:9) or the

Fear of Isaac (see Gen 31:42); the God of Jacob (see Ps 20:1) or the Mighty One of Jacob (see Gen 49:24). God, who was revealed to Abram as God Almighty (see Gen 17:1), was also known in various places by specific names: God Most High in Jerusalem (see Gen 14:18); God Everlasting at Beer-sheba (see Gen 21:33). Finally, the personal name of the God of Israel is Yahweh. Shortly before the Christian era, Jews, out of reverence, ceased pronouncing this personal name. When the consonants YHWH appeared, they would instead say *Adonai*, which is translated as "Lord." This form of reverence continues today even among Christians. When the word YHWH appears in the Hebrew text, for example, translators substitute LORD with upper case or capital letters. When the word is *adonai* it is written as Lord with lower case letters.

Finally, the dynamic power of God is referred to as the Spirit of the LORD. This is not a personal being as is the case in the Second or New Testament, but a principle of action. Although the spirit belongs to God, it is bestowed upon various individuals, but always for the sake of the whole community. It was the Spirit of the LORD that enabled the judges, the military leaders of Israel, to defeat their enemies (see Judg 3:10); that took possession of the kings and made them effective rulers (see 1 Sam 16:13); that enabled the prophets to proclaim the word of the LORD (see Mic 3:8). The prophet Joel proclaimed that in the time of fulfillment the Spirit would be given to all people, women and men alike, the young and the old, the free and the slaves (see Joel 2:28–29). One of the Christian writers described the experience of Pentecost as the time of the fulfillment of this prophecy (see Acts 2:17–18).

The Religion of the Israelites

Each period of Israel's history produced religious thinking and practices that reflected its social and political experience. It was during the tribal period that they developed laws that bound them together as a people under the sole leadership of God. These laws governed both their everyday life and their religious observances. The patriarchal organization of their society influenced the way they understood God's governance in their lives, and the wars that they fought in order to survive in a hostile world were thought to be sanctioned by the God who acted as their deliverer.

One of the reasons for the initial opposition to the monarchy was the way kings were perceived in the ancient Near Eastern world. They were thought to be either a god in human form or a direct descendant of some deity, and so many in Israel viewed them as rivals of the unique God with whom they had entered into covenant. It probably took a long time, but eventually Israel was able to reinterpret the understanding of monarchy so that there was no doubt about the human character of the king or about his accountability to God and to the law of Israel (see 2 Sam 7:8–17). Besides the administration of the realm and its protection against enemy forces, it was the king's responsibility to construct a temple to the deity. Although David planned to do so, it was his son Solomon who finally built the Temple in Jerusalem (see 1 Kgs 6–7). This Temple became the center for sacrifice, prayer, and the celebration of religious festivals. Over the years these services became more and more elaborate, requiring a host of temple personnel. Priests and cultic prophets gained importance, sometimes even vying with the king for prominence.

Prophets acted as the conscience of the nation. Passionately committed to the covenant made with God, they called the disloyal back to fidelity, encouraged the faint-hearted to remain steadfast in their devotion, and generally kept alive the hopes of a better future. Prophecy flourished during the years of the monarchy and seemed to decline as a religious institution as the monarchy did. While occasionally prophets still arose during the later post-exilic period (after 536 B.C.E.), their number diminished and they seldom had the influence that earlier prophets continued to enjoy.

At the heart of Israel's religion was the idea of covenant. Covenants were established between gods and the people or between kings and the people. Some were unilateral: only one partner having obligations toward the other (God promises to give Abram descendants and land, but asks for nothing in return, see Gen 15:1–6). Other covenants were bilateral, with both partners having obligations (God makes promises to Abram and requires that Abram and his male offspring be circumcised, see Gen 17:1–14). Several covenants are mentioned in the First Testament: between God and all of creation (see Gen 9:8––17); between God and Abram and his descendants (see Gen 15:18–21; 17:1–14); between God and the people at Mount Sinai (see Exod 31:12–17); between God and the family of David (see 2 Sam 7:12–16). The theology at the basis of these covenants continues to be important for Jews and Christians alike even to our day, for they show God's love for and ongoing relationship with humanity.

In the bilateral covenants, the obligations of the human partners were usually codified as law. This Law was thought to be directive rather than restrictive. It laid out the manner of living required of one committed to God in covenant. Such obligations were both vertical, pertaining to responsibilities toward God ("You shall have no other gods before me," Exod 20:2), and horizontal, pertaining to responsibilities toward other covenant partners ("You shall not steal,"

14

Responsibility toward God

Resp. toward other Covenant Partners

Exod 20:15). The Israelites believed that their laws, even their social laws, were sacred, given to them by God. Therefore, being faithful to social laws was seen as a religious act.

The ancient Israelites developed formal structures of worship, which included various forms of sacrifice. Most of the sacrifices in some way represented their dependence upon God for their very lives. This was particularly true of animal sacrifice. The lifeblood of sheep or goats or bulls, animals upon which they depended for survival, was offered in substitution for their own lifeblood. During various festivals they also offered the first fruits of their crops, as well as grains and oils. These practices were signs of their gratitude for life, their repentance for having violated their covenant commitment, or their need for God's assistance.

The basis of Israel's liturgical celebrations was the weekly Sabbath. There are two traditions that explain the reason for refraining from secular pursuits on that day. One requires that the Israelites rest in imitation of God who rested after having created for six days (see Exod 20:8–11). The other explains that their rest must be shared by the slaves who live among them. This should remind the Israelites that they, too, had once been slaves (see Deut 5:12–15).

Most of Israel's major feasts were seasonal in origin. The three principal ones were Passover and the Feast of Unleavened Bread, the Feast of Weeks or Pentecost, and the

Feast of Tabernacles or Ingathering. These were pilgrimage feasts, times when Israelites went to Jerusalem for their observance whenever this was possible.

Passover probably originated among nomadic people who broke camp in the spring in order to look for new pasturage. The sacrifice of a young animal was meant to ward off evil spirits and to ensure fertility of the flock. Unleavened Bread marked the beginning of the barley harvest. During the harvest celebration only bread made of the new grain was eaten. Eventually the celebrations of Passover and Unleavened Bread became one and were given historical meaning. The evil spirit was now seen as the angel of death that went through Egypt sparing every Hebrew household that had the blood of a lamb sprinkled on its doorpost but killing the firstborn of those Egyptian households that did not. Since the Israelites were prepared for an immediate escape from Egypt, there was no time for the bread to rise. This became the reason they ate unleavened bread during the time of the celebration.

The Feast of Weeks is celebrated about fifty days later, hence the name Pentecost. Although it originally marked the wheat harvest, it, too, soon took on historical significance. Its occurrence was believed to coincide with the anniversary of the date when Israel arrived at Mount Sinai, and so it became the feast that commemorated the Sinai covenant and the giving of the Law. The Feast of Tabernacles was celebrated as the climax of the agricultural year, the time when all of the crops had been brought in. To facilitate the harvesting, the people lived in the fields in temporary huts or tabernacles. This practice was soon interpreted as a commemoration of the time when the people lived in huts in the wilderness after their escape from Egypt. Over the years the agricultural origins of the festivals lost their importance and the historical interpretations took precedence. The celebration of many of these feasts is still alive in the religions of Judaism and Christianity.

Questions for Reflection: *Which period in ancient Israel's history do you think was the most interesting? Why? How has your personal history shaped the way you view the world and the people within it? Which images of God found in the First Testament do you find most comforting? Most challenging? Why, do you think, are there so many ways of representing God?*

Chapter 2

The Ancestors

All people have stories about their ancestors. Theses stories are more than mere history. They are stories of identity. They tell the people who they are, where they come from, why they are where they are, and what is expected of them. Many of us have either lost our ancestral narratives or have discounted them as irrelevant. Ancient Israel certainly did not. They preserved these traditions even when some of them seemed to conflict with or repeat others. The actual historical facts may be too deeply buried in the past to date accurately, but the stories have survived.

The collection of Israel's ancestral record begins with stories of characters who, strictly speaking, are ancestors not only of Israel but of all humanity. These stories are ancient explanations of what happened even before history as we know it had come to be remembered and recorded, stories of the human race before it divided into tribes and nations. These are accounts of primordial events that ultimately determined how human history would unfold.

The four primary ancestors are Abraham, Isaac, Jacob, and Joseph. Because this was a patriarchal (*patēr*—father, *archē*—head) society, women did not normally hold the same places of importance in society as did men. Although the wives of these patriarchs played significant roles in the traditions, strictly speaking they cannot be considered matriarchs (*mētēr*—mother, *archē*—head) because they were not in the principal ruling positions.

Although the stories of the various ancestors unfold in a way that suggests chronological order with physical descent of the characters, they probably originated independent of one another and were gradually brought together into one story as various clans or tribes joined with others. Today, through careful analysis of differences in language, customs described, and theology drawn, scholars have been able to distinguish two different ancestral traditions. The oldest is called the *Yahwist,* because of its frequent use of the divine name "Yahweh." The second is called the *Elohist,* because it refers to God as "Elohim," which means "gods." Although they do not contain ancestral narratives, two other traditions have been differentiated. One tells stories that interpret events from the perspective of the Law and is thus called *Deuteronomistic,* which means "second law." The fourth shows a preference for things cultic or liturgical and is referred to as the *Priestly* tradition.

Adam: Man from the Ground (Genesis 1–3)

The story of Adam and Eve is a story about origins. Such stories are concerned not merely with the events that happened in that "time before time," however, but with those events that originally shaped the dynamics of human history. In other words, the stories tell us not only where human beings came from but also why we seem to have a love-hate relationship with the earth, why women and men both long for each other and yet are sometimes alienated from each other.

Such stories are etiological (attempting to explain causes) rather than factual. They employ elements of what scholars call *myth*, a type of narrative that deals with realities whose scope is much broader than mere discernible data. Contrary to what many people commonly understand, myth recounts profound existential truth. The stories found in the opening chapters of the Bible, for example, are stories about "Everyman" and "Everywoman." They describe something about all of us.

There are two versions of the creation of the first couple. In the first one (see Gen 1:27–28), which is a very tight poetic construction, the man and the woman are created at the same time, and both are created in the image of God. Contrary to what some believe, *image of God* does not stand for the immortal soul. The people of the ancient world frequently set up images of their kings or their gods. These representations may have deteriorated into idols that were themselves worshiped, but that was not their purpose. Rather, they served as some kind of physical symbol that indicated where the king or god reigned supreme (something comparable to a national flag). The image was not considered the king or god, but a symbol of that individual's sovereignty. To say that the first man and woman were made in the image of God is to say that they were symbols of God's sovereignty in the world; they represented where God, not they, ruled supreme.

According to the second version, the man and the woman were created at different times, in different ways, out of different material (see Gen 2:4a–25). Several literary features mark this as an imaginative story rather than a factual account. Chief among them is the play on words found there. The man (*'ādām*) was made first, formed by God out of the dust of the ground (*'adāmâ*); the woman (*'iššâ*) was shaped from a rib of the man (*'îš*; a second word for man). A third play on words is found in an earlier Sumerian creation story. (The Sumerians lived from 2900–2360 B.C.E. in what today is Iran.) There the name of the creation goddess Ninti can mean "Lady of the rib" or "Lady of life." Although the play on words is lost when the account is translated into Hebrew, the storytellers of Israel retained the image of the rib and included a reference to life in the name Eve, Mother of the Living.

The poetic character of the account is also seen in the reference to "bone and flesh." Built from the man's rib, the woman certainly was his bone, but the word-pair is an example of a particular poetic pattern that expresses something in its totality. For example, the expressions flesh and blood, young and old, east and west, all set the limits with the words of the phrase, but are meant to include everything that exists between them as well. Bone and flesh refer to power and limitation respectively and, in this poetic form, suggest the total range of human potential. The woman is the man's strength and his weakness, and everything in between. From the very beginning, the man and the woman belong together. They are of the same bone and flesh, they are husband and wife, they complete each other.

The Bible first mentions death in this account of beginnings. There we read that God warned that if the original couple were to eat of the tree of knowledge of good and evil, they would be doomed to death. Belief that death is the punishment for sin grew out of this part of the story. However, if we read carefully, we discover that the first man was made of the dust of the ground, a clear reference to the ground of the grave. This suggests that he was destined for death from the very beginning. Furthermore, the punishment meted out for sin was said to endure only *until* death (see Gen 3:16–19). The story actually recounts how humankind was made of the stuff of the grave (dust) yet given access to a mysterious source of life (the tree of life in the garden). Not satisfied being dependent on God, the man and the woman took things into their own hands, sinned, were subsequently denied access to the tree of life, and were thus made subject to the consequences of mortality.

The separate and dissimilar punishments for the man and the woman, although probably descriptions of life in ancient Israel, are related to the account of their distinctive creations. The man suffers in relation to the ground from which he was formed; the woman suffers in relation to the man out of whose rib she was shaped. After their sin, life was fraught with pain for both the man and the woman, and this pain touched the very core of their beings. The same Hebrew word translates as the "pain" of pregnancy and the "toil" of farming. It is clear that their punishments were related to conditions of life, not death.

After their sentence had been passed and punish meted out, God gave this first couple another chance. Although they were driven out of the Garden of Eden, they were equipped to deal with the challenges of life. They would have to learn from the hard experience of life, but they would learn. They now knew that disregard of the directives of God would result in punishment, perhaps very severe punishment. However, they also came to know that the love of God far outstrips any failure of which they might be guilty. Like every child born into the human race from this point on, Adam and Eve would have to face uncertainties with trust, danger with courage, failure with humility, and all things with commitment to God.

Abraham: The Father of a Multitude (Genesis 12–20)

The story of Israel's ancestors begins in the area of the Tigris and Euphrates Rivers, in the area of what is modern Iran. Tradition reports that a man known as Abram was called by God to leave his home and to go to another land, a land in which God would make him progenitor of a great nation (see Gen 12:1–3). Abram took his family and possessions and traveled to this foreign land. There God made a solemn pact with him, promising him a multitude of descendants who would inherit the land promised. Abram's openness to God's call and his trust in God's promise have since become a model after which other believers are invited to pattern their lives.

This trust in a promise of descendants is particularly significant because Abram and his wife, Sarai, were childless, and they were already advanced in years. In an attempt to remedy their childlessness, as was the custom in those days, Sarai gave her slave girl, Hagar, to Abram to bear a child. (It seems that, like most ancient people, the early Israelites had foreign slaves.) Abram and Hagar had a son whom they named Ishmael, which means "Let God hear." However, God announced that it was important that the child of promise not be born of a slave but of a free woman. To assure Abram of the fulfillment of this promise, his name was changed to Abraham, which means "Father of a Multitude," and Sarai's name was also changed, to Sarah, which means "princess."

One day three men approached Abraham's tent. After he extended to them the customary courtesies of hospitality, they told him that Sarah, even in her old age, would bear a son who would be the fulfillment of God's promise. Sarah heard this and laughed. When the child was eventually born he was called Isaac, which means "May God laugh." Isaac and Ishmael became rivals, but eventually Isaac won out as the favored one. This child became the rival of Ishmael, a rivalry that was settled in Isaac's favor. Much later the similarity yet difference between these two sons served as an allegory for St. Paul, who contrasted the Jews and the Christians, since both religious groups claimed to be descendants of Abraham (see Gal 4:21–31).

In order to avoid disputes over grazing land, Abraham had given his nephew Lot a portion of land in the plain of the Jordan River. Lot and his family settled near the southern end of what has come to be known as the Dead Sea, in the vicinity of Sodom and Gomorrah. These cities became notorious for their depravity, a depravity that threatened to spread and infect the entire region. The only way to prevent this would be to utterly destroy them. Fearing that the innocent would be destroyed along with the guilty, Abraham pleaded with God to spare the cities. God agreed to do so if fifty righteous people could be found. Abraham bargained: What if there were only forty-five? or forty? or thirty? or twenty? or ten? Only six righteous people were found—Lot and his wife, his two daughters and their husbands—and so the cities were destroyed by fire and the land was purified. An interesting legend reports that out of curiosity, Lot's wife looked back at the burning cities and was transformed into a pillar of salt. This story has been used to explain the salt formations that exist even today in that part of the land.

Perhaps the best-known story about Abraham recounts his willingness to sacrifice his son Isaac. For several reasons, the contemporary reader will probably find this a difficult story to understand. First, it is God who commands Abraham to perform the sacrifice. We might wonder how a good God could make such a demand of a father. Furthermore, Isaac was the child of promise. Why promise Abraham a son and then require that he put him to death? The biblical text clearly states that God was testing Abraham. The reader may know this, but Abraham certainly did not, and so it almost seems that God is playing with Abraham. Second, how could a father agree to such a thing, especially when all of his hopes for the future rested on that particular son? But then, this is precisely the point of the narrative. It is not a story about the insensitivity of God, but of the total faith and trust of Abraham.

Isaac was not only a beloved son; he was the future of the entire clan of Abraham. With no one to carry on Abraham's name or inherit his property and possessions, not only would the clan cease to exist, but all trace of it would disappear from memory. While the contemporary reader might be concerned about the welfare of the individual Isaac, a more traditional person will realize the broader consequences for the whole people. As harsh as the command may appear to be, God is giving Abraham an opportunity to show that just as he entrusted his own future to God when he left his home and journeyed to a foreign land, so now he entrusts the future of his entire clan to God. If God could bring life out of a man and woman as old as Abraham and Sarah, surely God could ensure the future of this people. The story has a happy ending. Abraham demonstrated his faithfulness to God by taking the necessary steps to sacrifice Isaac, and the faithfulness of God was demonstrated when, at the last moment, Abraham was prevented from completing the horrible deed. At the end of the ordeal, God repeated the promise to bless Abraham with offspring as numerous as the stars in the heavens and the sand on the seashore (see Gen 22:15–18).

The Abraham tradition contains the beginnings of several themes that continue to be important in the religions of Judaism and Christianity. The first is the idea of *call*. God calls Abram and asks him to leave behind what he knows, and to trust in a God who makes promises. This leads us to the idea of the *promise* itself. In the stories, God promises prosperity and innumerable descendants to enjoy it. Finally, the tradition presents a *personal God* who is interested in and committed to the welfare of the people.

Isaac: The Laughter of God (Genesis 21–24)

Before he died, Abraham made sure that Isaac married a woman from his ancestral country. Since the Canaanites, the original inhabitants of the land given by God to Abraham, worshiped many gods, intermarriage with them might have weakened the commitment of Abraham's people to their own God. Rather than risk this, a servant was sent back to the home of a relative of Abraham, and there he found a suitable wife for Isaac. Her name was Rebekah. An arrangement was made with her father and her brother, a common custom in patriarchal societies. What is interesting is that they did not force the girl into the marriage. Rather, they first asked her if she agreed with the arrangement. Only after she consented did they begin making plans for her journey back to Abraham, there to become the wife of Isaac.

There is an interesting feature to each of the stories of the three ancestors: Abraham, Isaac, and Jacob. They were all married to women who at first were unable to conceive and bear children. Sarah was advanced in years (see Gen 18:11) and both Rebekah and Jacob's wife, Rachel (who was his favorite of several wives), were barren (see Gen 25:21; 29:31). Yet, these are the women who eventually gave birth to the sons through whom the promises of God were fulfilled. This detail in the lives of the women was probably a way the tradition underscored the uncommon character of the heirs. Their extraordinary conceptions suggest that from the very beginning they were specially chosen by God.

Rebekah eventually conceived not merely one son, but two. These twins became the ancestors of two related yet very different people, the Israelites and the Edomites. The story of the birth of the twins is filled with symbolism. The firstborn was called Esau. He is described as having been red and hairy at birth. There is a play on the words *red*, his color at birth, and *Edom*, the land in which his descendants ultimately settled. He is also said to have been hairy. There is a second play

31

on that word and *Seir*, a mountain in Edom. Thus the description of Esau associates him with the land of Edom.

The second child was born gripping his older brother's heel, and so he was called Jacob or "Heel-Gripper." The name describes what became Jacob's tendency to take advantage of his brother, Esau. Isaac seems to have preferred the elder son, who was a hunter and a man of the field, while Rebekah favored the younger one, who was quieter but quite devious. Although very little is known about Isaac, he will forever be remembered as the son who was almost sacrificed by his father, and the father who was easily deceived by his son.

Jacob: The Heel-Gripper (Genesis 25–36)

Two stories describe the rivalry between Jacob and Esau. The first has to do with birthright and the second with patriarchal blessing. The birthright was the portion of inheritance that each son received. An inheritance was usually divided into as many parts as there were heirs, except that the eldest son received a double portion. This was probably because he was expected to care for the parents in their old age and he would need added resources for that. In the first story, Esau comes in from the fields famished. His desire for food is so great that he actually sells his birthright to his brother for some stew (see Gen 25:29–34). Most likely this story was intended to show the foolishness of the Edomites (descendants of Esau) who were rival neighbors of the Israelites.

Both Isaac and Rebekah play important roles in the second story. When Rebekah overhears Isaac making plans with Esau to bestow on him the ancestral blessing that Isaac had received from his father, Abraham, she calls Jacob in and devises a scheme to trick Isaac into granting the blessing to Jacob. While Esau is out getting game for the feast, Rebekah fixes food for Isaac, and Jacob disguises himself as Esau. Since in his old age Isaac has gone blind, he does not detect the ruse until Esau returns. By then the blessing has been given and, once again, Jacob has taken advantage of his brother. The Israelites must have enjoyed this story as well, for it portrays their ancestor as crafty while that of the Edomites as lacking in wit. Jacob did not always have the upper hand, however. When he returned to the ancestral homeland to get a bride for himself, he fell victim to the wiles of his uncle, Laban.

As he left his home to journey to the homeland of his ancestors, he spent a night at a place called Luz. In a dream he saw a ladder reaching from earth to heaven, and angels ascending and descending. The LORD stood beside Jacob and made the promise to him that had been made to Abraham and Isaac before him: "The land on which you lie I will give to you and to your offspring; and your offspring shall be like the dust of the earth, and you will spread abroad to the west and to the east and to the north and to the south; and all the families of the earth shall be blessed in you and in your offspring" (Gen 28:13–14). Then God promised to protect Jacob in his travels and to bring him back safely to this land of promise. Upon awakening, Jacob realized the holiness of the place where he had slept and had his dream, and so he renamed it Bethel, which means "House of God." After this, Jacob resumed his journey in search of a wife.

Jacob's destination was the house of Laban, the brother of his own mother Rebekah. Laban had two daughters, Leah and Rachel. Jacob desired Rachel, the younger, and agreed to work seven years for the right to marry her. When the wedding night finally arrived, he was tricked by Laban and given Leah, since it was the custom that the elder daughter was to be married first. Jacob had to work seven more years before he could marry the woman he really loved. Leah may have been unloved but she, not Rachel, was able to conceive and give birth. She herself gave birth to one daughter and six sons, and her maid Zilpah bore two more sons. Two sons were also born to Rachel's maid Bilhah. Finally Rachel herself was able to conceive, and she, too, bore two sons. However, she died while giving birth to the second one. These twelve sons of Jacob were the ancestors of the twelve tribes that eventually became Israel. Because Rachel was Jacob's beloved wife, the children she bore, Joseph and Benjamin, became his favorite sons, but this favoritism would eventually return to cause him great sorrow.

By the time Jacob was ready to return to the land that God had promised to Abraham and then to Isaac and finally to Jacob himself, he had quite a retinue of wives and children and servants and flocks. However, he knew that he would have to face Esau, the brother that he had cheated, and he had no idea of how he would be received. For this reason he sent everyone else ahead while he remained on the bank of the river Jabbok. There, throughout the night, he wrestled with a mysterious being. Although he was not beaten he was struck on the hip socket, an injury that resulted in a limp. It was at this time that his name was changed from Jacob, "Heel-Gripper," to Israel, "I have wrestled with God and have prevailed." Having been sobered by this experience, Jacob was ready to meet his brother. The meeting was amicable and so Jacob was able to settle his extensive family in the land of promise.

Telling such stories about their ancestors reveals something very interesting about the ancient Israelites. There was never any doubt in their minds about God's special interest in them. God had promised again and again that they would thrive as a people and that they would do this on their own land. Furthermore, they believed that, like Jacob, they were much more clever than their neighbors, a characteristic that would have been highly prized in a society that always had to face the possibility of extinction. Finally, in order to get along with others, this cleverness had to be tempered. God always seemed to provide some situation that would sober the people and remind them that any blessing that they enjoyed came to them from God and not from their own inventiveness.

The name *Israel* came to have unique significance for the people of God. It was not only the name given to their ancestor Jacob, but the entire nation was eventually known by this name, a name that the people continue to bear to this day. Furthermore, the land that had been promised also came to be known as Israel. For political reasons, the name of this land is disputed today. While contemporary Jews and those who support their land claims call it Israel, the Palestinians and those who support them insist that the land be known as Palestine. Israel continues to be a significant theological reference for both Jews and Christians.

The descendants of Jacob, otherwise known as the tribes of Israel, believed that they were the chosen people of God. After all, God had first called their ancestor Abraham, and had promised to make his descendants a mighty nation and to bless them with a land that they could call their own. Furthermore, God had renewed these promises down through the generations to Isaac and then to Jacob. This conviction, that being the chosen people of God, has remained with them to this day and has been interpreted by Christians to include them as well.

Joseph: The Dreamer (Genesis 37–50)

Jacob's beloved son Joseph is the subject of several very interesting and important stories. Two in particular are remembered. In order to show his love for Joseph, Jacob bought him a long robe with sleeves. (The Septuagint says that it was many-colored.) Jacob's favoritism would have been cause enough for his other sons to take offense at their younger brother, but Joseph himself added to their resentment. He shared with his family the dreams he had in which he saw his parents and his brothers show him extraordinary homage. In the first dream he saw a field of grain in which his sheaf rose above the others, and theirs all bowed down before it. In the second dream, his parents were the sun and the moon and his brothers were eleven stars, all of which bowed down before him. Although Jacob rebuked Joseph for telling such a tale, his bragging caused his brothers to turn against him and, when they had the chance, they sold him to some passing merchants. They then soaked his famous coat in the blood of a goat and brought it back to Jacob, who concluded that some wild animal must have killed his beloved Joseph. At last the brothers were rid of the dreamer and his insulting dreams.

Joseph was taken into Egypt, where he experienced both suffering and success. There the very same extraordinary powers that pitted him against his brothers enabled him to rise to prominence in the court of the pharaoh. Joseph had interpreted the dreams of one of his fellow prisoners and, when the pharaoh himself had some mysterious dreams, Joseph was called upon to interpret them as well. Joseph explained to the pharaoh that by means of two different dreams he was being warned of approaching famine. Seven years of want would be preceded by seven years of good harvests. He advised the pharaoh to appoint someone to oversee the storage of grain during the years of plenty so that there would be enough during the lean years. The pharaoh wisely chose the very man who had interpreted his dreams: Joseph the dreamer.

When the famine did come, it raged across the land of Egypt, reaching even into Canaan and affecting the family of Jacob. Hearing that there was grain in Egypt, Jacob sent his sons to purchase some. They had no idea that the man who had become the governor over the land, the one who was second only to the pharaoh himself, was the very brother they had hated, sold into slavery, and long considered dead. For his part, Joseph kept his identity secret, for he was concerned about three things: Were his brothers still the vicious men that they had been in the past? What had become of his blood-brother Benjamin? Was his father alive? Without betraying himself, Joseph discovered that his brothers had repented of their former ways. Furthermore, Benjamin was not only alive but was actually protected by the very brothers who had once endangered Joseph. And finally, yes, his father was indeed alive.

After he revealed his true identity to his brothers, Joseph arranged to have his father brought to Egypt. Although Jacob died in Egypt, he made his sons promise to have his bones returned to the land of promise, there to be buried in the place purchased by his grandfather, Abraham, the burial place of Abraham and Sarah, Isaac and Rebekah, and Jacob's own wife, Leah. This promise was made before Jacob died, but it would take generations before it was fulfilled. His burial was delayed, because the family of Jacob settled in Egypt and prospered there until a pharaoh rose to power who did not look kindly upon these foreigners. It was this later pharaoh who oppressed the Israelites so that God intervened to bring them out of Egyptian servitude.

The story of Joseph shows that God can bring good out of situations that are themselves quite evil. After he revealed himself to his brothers, Joseph assured them that, although they had meant him harm, "God sent me before you to preserve life" (Gen 45:5). Actually, this theme runs through the entire collection of ancestral stories. God can raise up a mighty nation through women who are beyond childbearing years (Sarah) or who are barren (Rebekah, Rachel). God can use apparent tragedies to ensure the prosperity of this people (the trickery of Laban, the bragging of Joseph). To quote an old proverb: God writes straight with crooked lines.

Questions for Reflection: *The primordial stories of creation have shaped the way we understand humankind. How has your interpretation of the stories of Adam and Eve shaped your understanding of gender relations? Of sin and death? Jews,*

Christians, and Muslims all claim Abraham as their father. How might we use this claim as we work for peace among these peoples? Jacob was known as a cheat and a trickster, yet God created an entire nation through him. Can you give examples of how God works wonders through people or institutions that are less than perfect?

Chapter 3

The Judges

The judges of Israel carried the justice of God into the lives of the people. While this was often executed in a legal fashion, during the time of the Israelites' occupation of the land it was frequently accomplished on the battlefield. In other words, the judges were often military leaders (circa 1220–1020 B.C.E.).

Many of the stories of the judges follow a very set pattern: 1) the Israelites sin; 2) as a punishment, God strengthens an enemy against them; 3) the Israelites cry to God for deliverance; 4) God raises up a judge (a military leader) who defeats the enemy and restores peace (see Judg 3:12–15). The cycle of sin, punishment, and repentance repeats, and each time another judge is raised up as deliverer.

The judges were considered religious leaders, and the storyteller demonstrates this belief by saying that they had been seized by the spirit of the LORD. This means that it was God's power that enabled them to perform wondrous feats, and all victories were God's victories.

There is another side to the conviction that the victories are God's victories. Ancient Israel seems to have believed that their battles were really God's battles, and that they were actually being led into warfare by God. From this conviction they developed the image of God as a warrior. While such a perception of God probably gave them courage when they needed it and made them realize their total dependence upon God, it has left us with a very disturbing understanding of God. The ancients may have justified their warfare in this manner, but we today certainly cannot, for we perceive both God and warfare in very different ways. This means that we will have to look carefully at the stories of the judges in order to discover what message they might have for us today.

Joshua: "Yahweh Has Saved" (Book of Joshua)

Joshua, whose name means "Yahweh has saved," is the one who led the people into the land that God had promised to their ancestors following the exile in Egypt. He made a name for himself as a successful military leader when, during their people's sojourn in the wilderness after they left Egypt, he led a contingent of men against a fierce desert tribe called the Amalekites. While Joshua fought, two men held Moses' hands up in prayer. The victory went to the forces of Israel. Joshua was later chosen as one of the twelve men sent to survey the land of Canaan, the land of promise. Ten of these men brought back negative reports and advised against attack. Only Joshua and Caleb advocated attack. As a consequence, only two men and their families entered the land of promise. All the others died in the wilderness. The story demonstrates the need to trust in God and not in one's own powers.

It was God who directed Moses to appoint Joshua as his successor. In the presence of Eleazar the priest, and before the whole congregation of the people, Moses laid his hands on Joshua and commissioned him as God had commanded him, and Joshua was believed to be filled with the spirit of wisdom. Then, before he died, Moses counseled Joshua: "Do not fear or be dismayed" (Deut 31:8). From this time on, God directed Joshua.

There seems to be some discrepancy in the stories of the conquest of the land. One account gives the impression that the Israelites forced their way into the land at Jericho and then launched three major campaigns: one further into the interior, one to the north, and one to the south. However, the stories in the Book of Judges suggest that their victories were not so swift or complete. This suggests that the continuous narrative that we have is really a collection of individual stories that were joined together at some time in history. This should not disturb us, for the point of the tradition is not the historical accuracy of the accounts but the power of God acting through the various military leaders.

Today there are at least four versions of how the occupation may have occurred. The first and probably the oldest theory is the one that a literal reading of the accounts provides, that is, the conquest of the Canaanite inhabitants by the invading Israelites. However, certain stories support another possibility. They suggest that, while there certainly was some fighting, most of the Israelite occupation was the result of peaceful infiltration or immigration. A third view

holds that there was great unrest among the Canaanite people themselves and, through a kind of "peasants" revolt, they
separated themselves from the city-state network under which
they had lived and aligned themselves with the Israelites, an
independently minded group that came out of the desert. In
both of these situations the Israelites ultimately took control
of the land.

The fourth view is the most recently proposed theory.
It maintains that the early Israelites were originally
Canaanites who quietly left their cities and moved to the
highlands where they ultimately organized themselves into
the tribes that we have come to know. In whatever way we
understand the actual occupation, the theological point is the
same: God promised this land to the Israelites, and ultimately
they took control of it.

Stories abound regarding the extraordinary feats that
the Israelites were able to accomplish under the leadership of
Joshua. Among them are the crossing over the Jordan
riverbed while the flow of the waters was suspended (see
Josh 3:9–17), the defeat of the Amorites where the sun stood
still (see Josh 10:1–14), and the defeat of the more powerful
city of Ai (see Josh 8:1–29). However, the battle that is so inti-
mately connected with the leadership of Joshua is the one at
Jericho. Clearly the story of this victory is less an account of
the actual historical events than it is a liturgical reenactment of

them. While there certainly are warriors involved, the major players seem to be the seven priests, each of whom has a trumpet made of a ram's horn. These priests go ahead of the sacred object known as the ark of the covenant as if it were being carried into battle. This quite unusual group marches around the city for six days, the priests blowing their horns. Then, on the seventh, they march around the city seven times. The seventh time, with the priests blowing their horns, the people shout loudly and the walls of the city fall flat.

As seems to be the case in every battle story, the actual events are less significant than their meaning. It is obvious that battles are not really won in this way. However, when people are victorious despite the fact that the odds seem to be against them, it is not unusual that they credit God with their success. This is probably the case here. Nonetheless, several of the features of the reenactment may have actual military grounding. We do know that the Israelites did carry the ark of the covenant into battle ahead of the fighting forces. This was a way of demonstrating that it was God who was leading the army. The sound of trumpets may have been used to frighten the enemy. However, seven would hardly make a difference in war, although they would be enough during a liturgical celebration. The initial silence of the people suggests that surprise played a major role in the actual victory. Therefore, the liturgical reenactment, which included elements from an actual battle, captured both the excitement of the event and its religious significance. It is God who gives victory, even in situations that appear to be doomed to failure.

Deborah: At the Hand of a Woman (Judges 4–5)

In one of the stories that report the Israelites' cry to God, the chief characters are women. The first is a woman by the name of Deborah, a woman who appears to have enjoyed a prominent position in the community. She is identified and described as both a judge and a prophetess (see Judg 4:4), roles that in patriarchal societies were normally assigned to men. Although she was married, she is not known exclusively as the wife of her husband, contrary to another characteristic of a patriarchal society. In fact, we know nothing about Deborah's husband, other than the fact that he was married to her. Scripture names her, however, and describes both her judging and prophetic roles. As judge, she sits under a tree where the Israelites come seeking her judgment. In her prophetic role, she delivers the command of the God of Israel to Barak, a commander of a force of ten thousand soldiers.

Hearing the directive that Deborah delivers, Barak agrees to go to battle only if Deborah accompanies him. Each one of these details is an unusual circumstance in a patriarchal society that valued the interests and activities of men more than those of women.

This narrative contains other unusual details. Barak was sent by Deborah against one of the Canaanite kings. When the battle turned in favor of the Israelites, Sisera, the commander of the Canaanite army, fled the battlefield and sought refuge in the tent of Jael, the wife of a man he thought was an ally of his king. According to the customs of the time, it was wrong for him to enter the tent of another man's wife, and so he himself set in motion the course of events that eventually ended in his own death. The events occur quite rapidly. Sisera enters Jael's tent, and she covers him with a rug; he requests water, and she gives him milk. He asks her to guard the door of the tent, and while he is sleeping, she drives a tent peg into his temple. The story may sound quite violent to us, but the Israelites would have delighted in a tale that recounted the defeat of a celebrated enemy warrior at the hand of an unpretentious woman. The words of Deborah are fulfilled: "The LORD will sell Sisera into the hand of a woman" (Judg 4:9).

This story illustrates a number of things. First, it is a demonstration of Israel's faith in God's care for them, particularly when they turn to God for protection or help. Second, it also shows that God works through individuals whom society may not consider important. In this case, God saves the people through the prophetic leadership of one woman and the bravery and wits of another. The story shows that God is not bound by the social customs of people, regardless of how sacred they might appear to be. In fact, many of the stories of the Bible show that God works wonders precisely through those one would least expect. It is a fascinating way of showing that the wonders come from God and not from the ingenuity or might of human beings.

Gideon: Show Me a Sign (Judges 6—8)

The story of Gideon is the story of another unlikely person through whom God worked. By his own account, Gideon admitted: "My clan is the weakest in Manasseh, and I am the weakest in my family" (Judg 6:15). This ought to be reason enough to look somewhere else for an agent of salvation. Not convinced that it was God who had called him and chosen him to deliver the Israelites from the power of the Midianites,

Gideon demanded: "Show me a sign that it is you who speaks with me" (Judg 6:17). And God obliged. However, one sign was not enough for Gideon. Each time God gave him a directive, Gideon required that God provide a sign to assure Gideon that it was indeed God who was speaking and that he, Gideon, was the one chosen by God to perform marvelous feats on behalf of the people of God.

This judge is almost a comic figure in the way he insisted that God accomplish the exploits that he, Gideon, devised. Finally, Gideon was satisfied and God could begin preparations to deliver the Israelites. The battle itself has a farcical quality to it. The Midianites were an oppressive force before which the Israelites did not seem able to stand. When it came time to end their oppression once and for all, God directed Gideon to send home all of the Israelite soldiers who were afraid. Twenty-two thousand left and only ten thousand remained. God next had Gideon take the remaining men to the river to drink. Those who cupped the water in their hands were sent home. The three hundred who lapped the water like dogs would be the force that God would use to defeat the Midianites. Once again the story is told in such a way that all would know that it was the power of God that won the day and not the skill or prowess of the Israelites.

When the people realized that Gideon had been so successful with such a limited number of men, some wanted to make him their king. This was the first instance of Israelites seeking to establish a monarchy within their midst. Gideon totally rejected this plan for, while he may have been puffed up by his accomplishments, his ego was not so inflated as to presume to rival the sovereignty of God.

Samson: Dedicated to God (Judges 13–16)

The story of Samson (see Judges 13–16) is more than an account of another judge. It is a saga or hero story of epic proportions. It tells the tale of a man who, even before he was born, had been consecrated to God as a Nazirite, an ancient penitential sect that neither drank wine nor cut their hair. Like the ancestral sons of promise, his mother had been barren until an angel of the Lord appeared to her and foretold the birth of the child, thus indicating the extraordinary nature of his career. As long as he was faithful to the stipulations of his consecration, Samson was blessed by God with phenomenal strength. But when he profaned his commitment by revealing that his strength was in his hair, he was punished by the loss of his strength. His exploits were legendary: he tore a lion apart barehanded; he caught three hundred foxes and set fire to their tails; he killed a thousand men with the jawbone of a donkey. Finally, when his hair grew back, which indicated that he had returned to his Nazirite commitment, his strength returned and he toppled a temple filled with Philistines who were offering sacrifices to their god, Dagon.

Many details found within the story of Samson reveal aspects of the theological thinking that lies behind it. There is the uncommon piety first of Samson's mother and then of Samson himself. His mother consecrated him according to the customs of the Nazirites and he normally observed them. The primary regulations required of the members of this sect included abstention from alcoholic beverages, refraining from shaving, and avoidance of contact with the dead. The first and the third regulations play no role in the stories about Samson. The shaving of hair, however, is pivotal to the tradition.

A second characteristic of the story is Israel's attitude toward other nations. At various times in their history, Israelites were forbidden to have any social dealings with people of another culture. This regulation was intended to prevent them from being influenced by the religious thinking or practices of another group. The fear was that such influence might threaten the integrity of their commitment to their own God. This fear was well grounded, for that is precisely what happened in the case of Samson. He married a Philistine woman, Delilah, who tricked him into revealing the source of his strength, which was his unshorn head of hair. Actually, his strength was not in the long hair itself, but in his observance of the Nazirite regulation regarding shorn hair. Although it was Delilah who actually cut his hair so that he would lose his strength, and she did it when he was asleep, it was Samson himself who revealed the secret and who ultimately was responsible for the outcome of his revelation. He had allowed his foreign wife to weaken his defenses. His vow was violated, and so God punished him with loss of strength. Samson ultimately destroyed the Philistine threat, but at the cost of his own life.

Samuel: Your Servant Is Listening (1 Samuel 1–12)

Samuel was a man who functioned in various capacities; today we would say that he wore many hats. He was one of the personnel who ministered at the shrine at Shiloh (see 1 Sam 3:1–18); he functioned as a judge (see 1 Sam 7:2–17);

and he was a prophet of God (see 1 Sam 3:20). As had been the case with so many of Israel's major leaders, Samuel's birth was miraculous, for his mother was barren. Like Samson, he was dedicated to the LORD as a Nazirite by his mother. When her son was just a young child, she brought him to the shrine at Shiloh and entrusted him to Eli the priest. It was there that he was called in the night by the LORD: "Samuel! Samuel!" Thinking that it was Eli who called him, he ran to him saying, "Here I am!" After this happened three times, Eli realized that it was God calling the boy, and he instructed him to reply: "Speak LORD, for your servant is listening!" (1 Sam 3:9). It was then that God revealed the punishment that would fall upon the house of Eli because of the sinfulness of his sons. This was the beginning of Samuel's remarkable career.

It was while he was ministering before the ark of the covenant that Samuel was called to be a prophet of God. The ark of the covenant was believed to be the place where God was especially present in the midst of the people. As such it was the center of Israelite worship both during the time they spent in the wilderness and when they had settled in the land. It led the people into the battles that secured for them the land of promise (see Josh 6:6–11). Once they were established there, the ark was installed in a prominent place at various shrines, primarily Gilgal (see Josh 7:6), Bethel (see

Judg 20:27), and Shiloh (see 1 Sam 3:3). When the Temple was built, the ark was permanently enshrined there.

The ark itself was a chest made of acacia wood, 3¾ feet long, 2¼ feet high and 2¼ feet wide. Carried by acacia poles that were inserted into gold rings attached at each of the four corners, it was inlaid with gold, both outside and inside. A solid gold slab rested on the top, upon which were erected two gold cherubim. Several precious religious articles were preserved within the ark: a copy of the stone tablets upon which were inscribed the Ten Commandments (see Deut 10:2); the rod of Aaron that had miraculously flowered (see Num 17:2–5); and some of the manna (bread) that had nourished the people in the wilderness (see Exod 16:4–5). It is understandable why the ark was so cherished by the people.

The Philistines were the principal threat to the tribes at the time of Samuel, and so it was to him that the people came for leadership in their need. He prayed to God and offered sacrifices in their behalf. It was also to Samuel that they came asking for a king. Against the idea at first, he was eventually directed by God to anoint Saul as the first king, and when Saul proved to be unworthy of that exalted position, it was Samuel who anointed David to take his place. In a very real sense, Samuel was a transition person, leading the people from tribal organization into the monarchy.

The stories of the judges may contain elements of saga or hero stories, but they also emphasize how important obedience to the Law was to the people of Israel. They believed that it determined success or failure in personal life as well as on the battlefield. The reason for this stemmed from the fact of their covenant relationship with God. They had entered into a solemn agreement, one that carried serious responsibilities for both themselves and for God. If they were faithful to their part of the bargain, God would be faithful and bless them. On the other hand, if they turned their backs on what they had promised, God would be forced to carry out the punishment to which they had agreed. In the stories of the judges we see the covenant in operation.

Questions for Reflection: *Who are some of the strong women who have inspired you? What traits do you most admire in them? Name some of the women who are influencing the face of the world today. How are they doing this? Every culture has hero stories, like the stories of Samson. Who are some of the heroes in the lore of your people? What do these stories tell you about yourself?*

Chapter 4

The Kings

The political realities of the ancient Near Eastern world forced Israel to move from tribal organization and the religion that fit it so well to a monarchy and royal theology. This meant that tribal leaders had to relinquish much of their power and most of their autonomy in favor of a central government that placed power in the hands of a king and the people with whom he chose to surround himself. The shift was no easier from the point of view of religion. Since in the ancient Near Eastern world kings were thought to be somehow divine, Israel had to interpret monarchy in such a way as to avoid that understanding. The political shift that was required may have been quite difficult, but it was not impossible. It is not uncommon that at times of crisis group government gives way to the leadership of one individual. However, the way Israel reshaped its theology is remarkable, retaining its understanding of covenant with one God yet accepting a human king.

Saul: The Man of God (1 Samuel 8–31)

The first king of Israel was Saul (circa 1020–1000 B.C.E.). He was probably more a military leader than an actual ruler. At the time of Saul, the Philistines posed a serious threat to the survival of several of the tribes. They were themselves a confederation of five cities; three of them—Gaza, Ashkelon, and Ashdod—were situated along the coast of what is today the Mediterranean Sea. The other two cities—Gath and Ekron— were somewhat inland. The Philistines had a monopoly in iron, which gave them both economic and military advantages. They not only pillaged Israelite cities, they actually captured the ark of the covenant (see 1 Sam 5:1–12). It soon became clear that if the tribes failed to come to one another's assistance, which seems to have happened quite frequently (see Judg 5:23), the unified Philistines would be able to conquer them one by one. Israel needed someone who could rally the troops around him. Into this situation stepped Saul of the tribe of Benjamin.

The role of Samuel in the selection of the king cannot be underestimated. He was recognized as the chief spokesperson of God and, therefore, the people looked to him for direction and leadership. The biblical narrative tells us that God's choice of Saul as king was revealed to Samuel (see 1 Sam 9:15), so when the prophet saw Saul, he anointed him (see 1 Sam 10:1). Saul seems to have been the kind of man who instilled confidence. What the people needed at this time was a strong military leader, and Saul certainly was that.

Saul, however, seems to have disregarded some of the customs of the time. Religious practice required that sacrifice be offered before one went into battle, and that only an approved religious person could officiate at such a sacrifice. This person was Samuel. On one occasion, he was quite late in coming to perform the prescribed ritual and so Saul took it upon himself to offer the sacrifice in Samuel's place (see 1 Sam 13:1–14). This disregard for religious observance was the beginning of Saul's decline. He ultimately lost favor with God and was replaced by David.

David: This Is the One
(1 Samuel 16–1; Kings 2)

As happened with the selection and anointing of Saul, so Samuel was the one who was told by God to choose a king from the family of Jesse of the tribe of Judah. Although Jesse brought seven of his sons before Samuel, none of them received the approval of God. Only when David, the youngest, was brought to the prophet did God say to him: "This is the one!" And so Samuel anointed him king even while Saul was still reigning. The relationship between David and Jonathan, Saul's son and presumed successor, is legendary. "Jonathan made a covenant with David, because he loved him as he loved his own soul" (1 Sam 18:3), even though Jonathan knew that David, not he, would succeed his father as the next king.

It was really David who consolidated the tribes into a unified nation (circa 1000–960 B.C.E.), and he did it in three steps. David and his followers had been driven out of the land of Israel by Saul, who had become envious of David's popularity as a soldier. Living on the outskirts of the southern desert, he defended some of the cities of the southern tribes of Israel, protecting them from the Philistines and even enriching them from what he had plundered from these long-time enemies of Israel. With the death of Saul, the people of the southern tribe of Judah, David's own tribe, called for him to be their king (see 2 Sam 2:1–7). After some time, the tribes of Israel in the north came to David with the same request (see 2 Sam 5:1–5), and he agreed. This made him both the king of Judah and the king of Israel. Finally, David and his men captured the Jebusite city-state of Jerusalem, making it David's own city by conquest. He was now the ruler of three quite independent political groups, and under him they gradually became one kingdom. However, despite this unification, neither the southern kingdom of Judah nor the northern kingdom of Israel would ever completely lose its own identity. They would eventually split after the death of David's son Solomon.

It was to David that the promise of a dynasty was made. The traditional story states that David planned to build a house (temple) for God, but was told through the prophet Nathan that, instead, God would build a house (dynasty) for David. God ratified this promise by entering into a covenant with David (see 2 Sam 7:12–16). The actual historical circumstances of this event are less important than the theological meaning of the tradition of God's promise to David, a tradition that has remained one of the most important theological themes of Jewish faith. It is a tradition that has been carried into Christian faith as well, for the earliest Christians understood Jesus as the son of David, the one through whom this promise was ultimately fulfilled.

Besides his theological significance, David was also remembered as a very colorful figure. In his youth he defeated the giant Goliath (see 1 Sam 17:38–51), demonstrating how faith in God is stronger than a coat of mail. His murder of a soldier named Uriah in order to cover his adulterous affair with Uriah's wife, Bathsheba, is known to all. The biblical story focuses on the guilt he experienced when Nathan the prophet condemned him for these crimes (see 2 Sam 11:1–12:14). The story of the intrigue within David's own family, as his sons vied with one another for the right to succeed their father as king, constitutes a significant section of two biblical books (see 2 Samuel 9–20 and 1 Kings 1–2). There we find the murder of one son, the treachery and death of another, and the attempt to seize the throne by a third. The family conflict is only resolved when Bathsheba, with the aid of the prophet Nathan, devises a plan to ensure the succession of her son Solomon. At the time of his death, David had reigned for forty years, forty years that saw an entirely new nation rise out of the tribal confederation.

Solomon: Beloved of the LORD (I Kings 2–11)

The Bible presents a picture of Solomon that is conflicting. On the one hand he is remembered as the king who built the magnificent Temple in Jerusalem, and he is regarded as the wisest of the wise. On the other hand his building projects severely taxed the people and, at his death, their dissatisfaction with the policies that he had instituted caused the northern tribes to separate themselves from the rule of the royal family. Solomon was the second son of David and Bathsheba—the first son, the one who was conceived during their adulterous affair, having died at birth, probably as a punishment for the initial affair. Besides the name Solomon, which comes from the same Hebrew root *shlom,* meaning "peace," he carried a second name, Jedidiah, which means "Beloved of the LORD." The accomplishments of David enabled Solomon to be born into a life of privilege and to inherit a well-established royal institution. He did not have to fight outside forces as his father David had. Instead, he could concentrate on internal matters.

The early stories about Solomon depict him as a man totally dedicated to God. At the beginning of his reign (circa 960–922 B.C.E.), he was given an opportunity to ask anything of God and it would be granted him. Solomon asked for the wisdom that would be needed to rule his people well. This greatly pleased God, who granted him wisdom and great wealth besides (see 1 Kgs 3:3–14). This wisdom was demonstrated again and again as Solomon decided various cases and increased his wealth and reputation through trade. However, it is the building of the Temple that really established him as a worthy ruler. Both the structure itself and the furnishings with which it was appointed dazzled the eye (see 1 Kings 6–8), providing proof of his wisdom, his commitment to God, and his extensive wealth.

It is interesting that the site of the Temple, that piece of land that was considered exceptionally sacred to the Israelites, has a long history of belonging to someone else. It began as the threshing floor of Araunah the Jebusite (a member of the Canaanite people who ruled in Jerusalem before David conquered it). Today it is occupied by the Arabs, who built the Mosque of Omar and the structure known as the Dome of the Rock.

The Temple itself was elaborately constructed with an entrance facing east, where the sun rises. The interior was divided into three sections, each section representing a deeper experience of the presence of God: the vestibule into which the Israelites could enter; the sanctuary where only priests had access; and the Holy of Holies in which the ark of the covenant was kept and into which only the high priest could enter. This magnificent edifice may have been the pride of the nation, but it was built by Israelites forced into conscripted work units. Men from all of Israel were obliged to work one month in Lebanon erecting buildings for the King of Tyre, and two months at home building the Temple, Solomon's own palace, and the walls of the city (see 1 Kgs 5:15–32).

This kind of forced labor was a heavy burden to bear for people who prided themselves in being God's chosen people, delivered from bondage in Egypt. Furthermore, Israelites being the forced labor for the construction of buildings for a foreign king suggests that Solomon was indebted to that king. This is perhaps a foreshadowing of the gradual decline of the once glorious kingdom of David. This sorry state became clear at the death of Solomon, when Rehoboam, his son and successor, went to the elders of the northern tribes seeking their allegiance. There he threatened them: "My father made your yoke heavy, but I will add to your yoke; my father disciplined you with whips, but I will discipline you with scorpions" (1 Kgs 12:14). In response, they declared their independence of the rule of the Davidic king and set up their own monarchy. Once again two kingdoms existed in the land:

the kingdom of Judah in the south and the kingdom of Israel in the north. The fruits of Solomon's poor leadership ripened for harvest.

Hezekiah: The Reformer (2 Kings 18–20)

The biblical writers were very critical of the kings. Every one of the rulers of the northern kingdom of Israel was condemned because "he did what was evil in the sight of the LORD, as his ancestors had done. He did not depart from the sins of Jeroboam the son of Nebat, which he caused Israel to sin" (2 Kgs 15:9). The sin referred to was the secession from allegiance to the Davidic king, which led to worship at shrines other than the major shrine in Jerusalem. The southern kings of Judah did not fare much better. It was said of most of them that "he did what was right in the sight of the LORD, yet not like his ancestor David" (2 Kgs 14:3). Only Asa (see 1 Kgs 15:11), Hezekiah (see 2 Kgs 18:3), and Josiah (see 2 Kgs 22:2) are given unqualified praise, the latter two because of the reforms they attempted to launch during their reigns.

Hezekiah (circa 715–686 B.C.E.) was king of Judah during part of the time that Isaiah and Micah ministered as prophets in Judah. He was twenty-five when he succeeded his father, and he ruled the southern kingdom for almost thirty years. He was very faithful to the Law and inaugurated a reform intended to cleanse the land of unclean practices of worship. He destroyed both the high places, which were open-air sanctuaries associated with Canaanite worship, and the sacred poles, which were phallic symbols that played an important role in Canaanite fertility cults. What might appear as merely a religious reform was actually a political move as well, for it told the Assyrians, of whom Hezekiah and his people were vassals, that they were taking their lives back into their own hands.

Assyria did not look kindly upon this move to reform, correctly seeing it as an act of defiance and a step toward independence. In response, King Sennacherib launched a military campaign against the kingdom of Judah. Hezekiah was able to save Jerusalem only at the price of a huge tribute paid to the Assyrian king. Sennacherib returned to finish his conquest, but unexpectedly ended his assault. Some think that affairs in Babylon necessitated his immediate return. Others believe that a plague broke out in his camp. Whatever the reason, Israel interpreted this as but further evidence of Jerusalem's special importance to God, an importance that is manifested in God's extraordinary protection. Throughout the period of Hezekiah's reign, the prophet Isaiah gave the king the same counsel that he had given the king's father, King Ahaz: remain neutral! Do not align yourself with either Egypt or Assyria! Place your trust in God! From Isaiah's point of view, the miraculous saving of Jerusalem was proof of God's care.

Josiah: No King Like Him (2 Kings 22–23)

The second great reforming king was Josiah, who became king when he was only eight years old. During his reign (circa 640–609 B.C.E.) a copy of the Law was discovered in the Temple and, influenced by the directives found in it, the king launched a comprehensive reform. He began with the purification of the Temple in Jerusalem; he pulled down shrines where inappropriate worship was conducted; he made Jerusalem central for the cult of the God of Israel; he commanded that the Passover be celebrated regularly. It was to Josiah that the highest praise was given: "Before him there was no king like him, who turned to the LORD with all his heart, with all his soul, and with all his might, according to the law of Moses; nor did any like him arise after him" (2 Kgs 23:25). This praise is taken directly from the tradition of the "great commandment": "You shall love the LORD your God with all your heart, and with all your soul, and with all your might" (Deut 6:5), one of the laws referred to by Jesus himself (see Matt 22:37; Mark 12:30; Luke 10:27).

Unfortunately, while still a young man, Josiah attempted to block the Egyptians who were marching north to assist the Assyrians, and he was killed in battle. With him died the reform he had initiated and the hopes that had grown up along with it. Not too long after his death, Judah was overrun by the Babylonians, the city of Jerusalem fell, and many of its leading citizens were taken into exile.

The kingdom that was born with Saul and that grew and thrived under David and Solomon was dismantled, never again to enjoy the glory and prestige of the past. However, God had made a covenant with David, and God's word was always true. The people may not have experienced independent rule under a king or, when they did, the king may have been a terrible disappointment, but God's word was always true. It was out of this confidence in the steadfastness of God's word that a form of *messianism* developed. This term comes from the fact that kings were anointed, and the Hebrew word for anointed one is "messiah." (Priests were also anointed and so a tradition about a priestly messiah grew up as well.) This explains why the people at the time of Jesus asked if he was the messiah, the son of David. They were hoping that he was the one who would overthrow the rule of their Roman occupiers and reestablish the independent kingdom of David. Jesus refused to be cast in this role. However, he did insist that he had come to establish a kingdom, the Kingdom of God.

We are indebted to the period of the kings for the royal theology that has shaped so much of our understanding of Christology. All of the hopes associated with the kingdom of David have been applied by Christians to Christ. However, this has not happened without their engagement of significant reinterpretation. We see this as early as the Gospels themselves. There we read that during Jesus' triumphant entrance into Jerusalem, the people acclaim him "son of David" (Matt 21:9; Mark 11:10), the "King of Israel" (John 12:13). They were probably understanding these titles in the traditional political way. However, when standing before Pilate, Jesus admits that he is indeed a king, but he insists that his kingdom is not of this world (see John 18:36). This announcement is in keeping with his teaching about the "Kingdom of God," teaching that is found in his parables. His is a kingdom that is deep within the hearts of women and men, not in their social or political structures. What has changed is not the idea of kingship, but the meaning of kingdom.

The way the theme of monarchy developed provides us with an insight into the ingenious process of interpretation and reinterpretation. First, in ancient Near Eastern thought, the king was believed to be a divine being, physically descended from the god and, therefore, the son of the god. Israel's faith rejected such a belief. Rather, it insisted that human beings, even kings, were merely human and neither divine nor some combination of the divine. Furthermore, its faith was monotheistic, giving allegiance to only one God. When monarchy became a political necessity, Israel retained some of the ancient Near Eastern principles of monarchy, but reinterpreted others. It acknowledged that the king did indeed enjoy a special relationship with God, a unique kind of covenant. However, the king was not ever considered a real "son of God." Rather, he was a member of the human community and was bound to obedience to the Law just like every other Israelite ("I shall be a father to him, and he shall be a son to me. When he commits iniquity, I will punish him with a rod such as mortals use, with blows inflicted by human beings," 2 Sam 7:14).

It seems that Israel emptied the monarchy of its divine character. The king may have been considered a "son of

God," but this was a title of office not a designation of descent. When we come to the Christian community, we see that the title "son of God" takes on new meaning, a meaning that is actually a return to the ancient meaning. Christian faith insists that Jesus is indeed the "Son of God," directly descended from God, sharing the nature of God. Where the faith of Israel emptied the title of its divine character, the Christian faith gave it back its original meaning.

Questions for Reflection: *Saul began with great hopes, but ended in tragedy. How can one fault destroy a person? What can be done to prevent this from happening? The Second Vatican Council was a time of church reform. However, the way it has been understood has also caused great upheaval. In what ways have you experienced this reform? In what ways have you experienced this upheaval?*

Chapter 5

The Prophets

Prophecy, understood not as the forecasting of the future but as the mediation and interpretation of the will of God, is a common phenomenon in most religions. Prophets are those who receive divine revelation, or interpret it, or both. They usually received the revelations through dreams, visions, or mystical experiences, or by the reading of signs, such as the way sticks fall when thrown into the air or the configuration of the entrails of animals. The phenomenon of prophecy in ancient Israel is traced back to Moses, who himself was considered the prophet—or spokesperson of God—

par excellence (see Deut 18:15). He was the one who first spoke the word of God.

Prophecy became more widespread during the time of tribal organization. As seen above, Deborah was considered a prophet, as were Elijah and Elisha. Probably the best-known prophets are those whose teachings were preserved by their followers and have come down to us today in books in the Bible that bear the names of the men themselves, for example, Amos, Hosea, Isaiah, Jeremiah, and Ezekiel.

At the heart of the teaching of each and every prophet is the theology of covenant. Israel had entered into a solemn agreement with God, and this agreement bound the people to a particular manner of living. The prophets encouraged the people in their commitment, reminding them of God's goodness in the past and assuring them that their fidelity would result in comparable blessings from God in the future. On the other hand, they denounced the people when they disregarded their covenant commitment and lived lives that were contrary to the will of God.

The message of the prophets was always relevant to their times. When the people were tempted to align themselves with a foreign nation, for example, one prophet called for unquestioning trust in God (see Isa 7:14–17). When the people who had returned from exile in Babylon postponed the rebuilding of the Temple, another prophet castigated them for this delay (see Hag 1:1–11). The prophets have been called the "conscience of Israel," and a study of their messages will show that this title was an appropriate one.

Moses: A Prophet Like Me

Most people think of Moses as a deliverer or a lawgiver rather than a prophet. However, if we remember that prophecy is a form of mediation and a prophet is one who speaks the word of God to the people (see Exod 4:12), then certainly Moses is a prophet. Furthermore, in the Book of Deuteronomy we find a very important promise. It is Moses who speaks: "The LORD your God will raise up for you a prophet like me from among your own people; you shall heed such a prophet" (18:15). Moses was indeed a spokesperson of God, but before he functioned in that way, his life took some interesting turns.

Born of Israelite parents living in Egypt, the infant Moses faced the peril decreed by the pharaoh "who did not know Joseph" (Exod 1:8). The infant was condemned to death along with all other male babies. Saved by his courageous sister, he was raised by the very daughter of the pharaoh who had sentenced him to death. It was not until he was an adult that he discovered his true identity; he was really an Israelite, a member of the oppressed people who were pressed into forced labor building supply cities. It was while he was tending the flocks of Jethro, his father-in-law, that God spoke to Moses from the midst of a bush that burned but was not consumed. He had been chosen to lead the oppressed people out of Egyptian bondage. Boldly, Moses asked for the personal name of this deity who was calling him to such a momentous task. The only name that he was given was: "I AM WHO I AM." The exact meaning of this name has puzzled scholars to our day. It is interesting to note that the man who would eventually become the spokesperson of God claimed that he was not the man for the task because he lacked eloquence. In response to this, God appointed Moses' brother Aaron to speak for him.

The story of pharaoh's defiance of God's wishes is well known. Even a series of devastating plagues did not move him in his obstinacy (see Exodus 7–10). It took the death of the firstborn son of every Egyptian family, including the pharaoh's, to force the release of the Israelites. Their mysterious deliverance from the sword of the angel of death and their miraculous crossing of the Sea of Reeds are commemorated every year in the celebration of the Passover. Moses was the intermediary through whom God spoke to both the pharaoh and the Israelites; he was the one who led them out of Egypt, across the dry seabed, and into the wilderness beyond. The one who had been raised in the house of the pharaoh had now escaped it—taking along with him his own frightened people.

While in the wilderness, Moses continued to be the one through whom God spoke to the people. He is the one who told them that God would feed them with quail at twilight and in the morning with manna, a kind of fine flaky substance that took the place of bread (see Exodus 16; Numbers 11). It was Moses who struck the rock that brought forth water to refresh the complaining people (see Exod 17:1–7; Num 20:1–13). Although Moses acted as their leader, it was really God who, through a cloud by day and a pillar of fire by night, led the people through the wilderness to the foot of Mount Sinai (see Exod 13:17–22; Num 9:15–23).

It was at the mountain that events occurred that would transform this motley group into a people with an identity and a purpose. Once again it was Moses who approached God and it was to Moses that God's words were delivered. The story recounts how a covenant was made on that day. The ceremony followed the ancient covenant format (see Exod 20:2–17): the deity is named ("I am the LORD your God"); past favors are recounted ("who brought you out of the land of Egypt"); the resulting obligations are decreed

("You shall . . . You shall not . . ."); blessings for the observance of these regulations and punishment for violation of them are listed (Deuteronomy 28-29). Although these obligations have come to be known as the Ten Commandments, the Jews also refer to them as the Ten Words. Moses delivered God's words to the people, words that will mark them forever as the People of God. These Ten Words are a basis of the ethical life of both Jewish and Christian believers.

Although he never entered the land to which he led the people, Moses continued to influence both their lives and their hopes. The passage quoted earlier from Deuteronomy is evidence of this: "The LORD your God will raise up for you a prophet like me from among your own people; you shall heed such a prophet" (18:15). This passage took on eschatological (future or endtime) significance in the thinking of Israel. Although it was variously interpreted over the years, it soon was associated with the mysterious Elijah who was taken up to heaven in a fiery chariot, to return before the end of days (see Mal 4:5). At the time of Jesus, many of the people were convinced that he was this prophet returned (see John 1:21; 6:14). Peter, newly made bold when the Spirit descended upon the early Christian community, preached that Jesus was indeed this eschatological prophet (see Acts 3:17–26).

Amos: Woe to You (Book of Amos)

Amos (circa eighth century) is the first of what have come to be known as the classical prophets, prophets whose teachings have been preserved for us in collections identified by their own names. Although he was from Tekoa, a small town in the southern kingdom of Judah, Amos traveled to the northern shrine of Bethel to deliver his scathing message. Prophets were called from various walks of life, and Amos identifies himself as a herdsman and a dresser of sycamore trees (see Amos 7:14).

At the time of Amos, the northern kingdom was quite prosperous and, as is so often the case, their very prosperity led the people into moral corruption. The specific way the people of Israel violated their covenant responsibilities was through social injustice perpetrated against their own people. Their sins called down upon them the wrath of God, and Amos was chosen to deliver this message. His harsh words were directed particularly against the political and religious leaders, the king and the priests. He condemned the inequities that existed with words that were straightforward and piercing, calling the pampered women of the upper class "cows of Bashan" (Amos 4:1).

This prophet uses a very interesting form in his condemnations of various neighboring nations, a kind of numerical form (x + 1): "For three transgressions of Damascus, and for four . . . for three transgressions of Gaza and for four . . . for three transgressions of Tyre and for four" . . . etc. (see Amos 1:3, 6, 9). It seems that the prophet is tracing a circle, beginning with Gaza in the southwest and moving clockwise until he completes the circle with the southern kingdom of Judah. The Israelites must have taken great delight in the prophet's words. The nations that he condemns had inflicted unspeakable suffering upon the citizens of the northern kingdom. This delight was complete when the southern kingdom was condemned as well. The prophet, however, was not finished. He then pointed his accusing finger at the northern kingdom, the very people in whose midst he stood, for they too had sinned, selling the righteous for silver, prostituting themselves at the altars of other gods. The kingdom of Israel was not spared the wrath of God.

It appears that the people actually did observe the cultic celebration of the festivals; they did offer fatted animals in accord with the Law. However, God was not pleased with their sacrifices; God was not interested in their songs. In place of correct cultic performance, God said: "Let justice roll down like waters, / and righteousness like an everflowing stream" (Amos 5:24). This teaching underscores one of the most significant aspects of ancient Israelite religion, that is, the connection between one's covenant commitment to God and one's covenant responsibilities toward other covenanted neighbors.

Hosea: You Are My People (Book of Hosea)

The covenant between God and the people is succinctly expressed in a very short phrase: I am your God; you are my people! This was a technical phrase and was not taken lightly. The message of the prophet Hosea describes the dissolute state of the people by playing with this most significant phrase. Like Amos before him, Hosea (circa eighth century) preached to people in the northern kingdom but, in this instance, this was the kingdom to which the prophet himself belonged. Hosea was concerned with his own people's disregard of their covenant commitment, and he used his own family situation to describe this sorry state of affairs.

The text tells us that the prophet's wife, Gomer, was unfaithful to him. We are not sure whether this meant that she was involved with other men or was attached to one of the nearby shrines and functioned there as a cult prostitute. Whichever the case may have been, she was guilty of adulterous behavior. She bore three children, the names of two being of special interest to us here. The second child was a girl and the prophet named her *Lō-rūhamah*, which means "Not pitied," for God "will no longer have pity on the house of Israel or forgive them" (Hos 1:6). The third child, a son, was named *Lō-ammī*, "Not my people" (Hos 1:9). Just as Gomer had violated her marriage commitment, so had Israel been unfaithful to its covenant relationship. Following this metaphor, one could say that Israel had played the prostitute with other gods and, as a result, God declared that the children born of her were "not my people," and would be "not pitied."

How would Hosea/God regain the love and commitment of Gomer/Israel? "I will allure her, / and bring her into the wilderness, / and speak tenderly to her" (Hos 2:14). Since the wilderness was the place where the covenant was first made, it is fitting that the wilderness be the place where it is remade. There in the wilderness, a new covenant is made "with the wild animals, the birds of the air, and the creeping things of the ground" (Hos 2:18). The language is reminiscent of the first creation story in Genesis, suggesting that this is indeed a new creation and the children are born anew: "I will have pity on *Lō-rūhamah*, / and I will say to *Lō-ammī*, 'You are my people'; / and he shall say, 'You are my God'" (Hos 2:23).

Despite the negative feminine image that plays such a large role in the book, the primary religious message of the prophet is the compassionate mercy of God. Whether the prophet uses the metaphor of an unfaithful wife or an unfaithful husband, it is clear that God's love is steadfast and will not be conquered by infidelity. God continues to love and to forgive; God never tires of entering anew into a covenant of intimate commitment.

Isaiah: The Spirit of the LORD (Book of Isaiah)

The biblical book that is ascribed to the prophet Isaiah gives evidence of having been written during three very different periods of time. This implies that not all of it could have been written by the prophet himself (circa eighth century). All scholars agree that there are at least two major divisions: chapters 1–39, which contain the teachings of the prophet himself; chapters 40–66, which are attributed to an unknown disciple referred to as Second or Deutero-Isaiah. Today most scholars divide the second half of the book into two sections as well. Chapters 40–55 retain the name Second or Deutero-Isaiah (circa early sixth century); chapters 56–66 come from the pen of yet another disciple known as Third or Trito-Isaiah (circa late sixth century). We have already seen how complicated the question of biblical authorship can be. This is a good example of how disciples, who may never have known the prophet himself, interpret his teaching for their own time and determine to confer the prophet's authority on that teaching.

The actual prophet Isaiah ministered in the southern kingdom of Judah years before Jerusalem fell to the Babylonians. His teaching was based on the conviction that God is all-holy and all-powerful. This conviction was forged during his experience of a vision of God that took place in the Temple, the vision that inaugurated him into his prophetic ministry. There he saw God seated on a throne surrounded by angels who sang out: "Holy, holy, holy is the Lord of hosts; / the whole earth is full of his glory" (Isa 6:3). It was this very conviction of God's power that explains the political neutrality that he counseled for King Ahaz (see Isa 7:14–17) and later for his successor King Hezekiah (see Isa 37:5–7). According to Isaiah, there was no need to enter into alliances with other kings in order to stave off attack by Assyria. Rather, he believed that God would control Assyria in ways that Israel and the other nations could never even begin to imagine. Some might say that the prophet was politically naive; others would credit him with extraordinary trust in God.

It was not that Isaiah disdained the monarchy; quite the contrary. He had the highest regard for it, even though he may have questioned the wisdom or commitment of the ruling monarch. Some of the most beautiful messianic poetry comes from Isaiah:

> For a child has been born for us,
>   a son given to us;
> authority rests upon his shoulders;
>   and he is named
> Wonderful Counselor, Mighty God,
>   Everlasting Father, Prince of Peace (Isa 9:6).

> A shoot shall come out from the stump of Jesse,
>   and a branch shall grow out of his roots.
> The spirit of the LORD shall rest upon him,

> the spirit of wisdom and understanding,
> the spirit of counsel and might,
> the spirit of knowledge and the fear of the LORD.

> His delight shall be in the fear of the LORD
> (Isa 11:1–2).

Isaiah probably hoped that he would live to see this exceptional king. Although he did not, Israel kept alive the hope of such a ruler. The early Christians found the fulfillment of such hope in the person of Jesus. For this reason, these passages continue to play an important role in our celebration of Christmas, the time when we rejoice in the birth of the messianic king.

The prophet known as Second or Deutero-Isaiah spoke to a people who had been broken by the experience of the Exile. It may have been true that they had brought that terrible ordeal upon themselves by their sins. However, they had paid the price for their infidelity and finally it was time for them to be encouraged, to be reminded that their God had led their ancestors through the wilderness into a land flowing with milk and honey. That same God would now grant them the same favor; they would be led through a kind of wilderness back to the land that had been promised to them so long ago. This prophet cried out:

Comfort, O comfort my people,
   says your God.
Speak tenderly to Jerusalem,
   and cry to her,
that she has served her term,
   that her penalty is paid,
that she has received from the LORD's hand
   double for all her sins (Isa 40:1–2).

The message of this prophet is one of encouragement rather than warning. He speaks of springs in the wilderness, of a new creation. He also describes the mysterious Servant of the Lord (Isa 42:1–7; 49:1–7; 50:4–9; 52:13–53:13), who is totally committed to God despite the suffering that this commitment costs him, a mysterious figure who lends the Christian community yet another image for understanding Jesus.

Finally, an unnamed prophet, perhaps Third or Trito-Isaiah, announces the arrival of the time of fulfillment, the year of the Lord's favor (Isa 61:1–3). The expression is probably an allusion to the jubilee year, a time of significant economic realignment. In the Book of Leviticus we find an injunction directing that every fiftieth year should be celebrated as jubilee, a time when debts were forgiven, when property was returned to the original owners, when indentured slaves were set free, when even the land was allowed to rest and lie fallow (see Lev 25:8–55). Whether this practice was ever followed, the idea of jubilee soon came to represent the time of fulfillment, the time when everyone had what she or he needed to live a decent life and there was no more poverty or oppression.

It was this passage from Isaiah that Jesus read when he was handed the scroll in the synagogue of Nazareth (see Luke 4:16–18). It was of this idea of jubilee that he spoke when he told those listening to him: "Today this scripture has been fulfilled in your hearing" (Luke 4:21). In this way, Jesus announced the arrival of the time of fulfillment. By identifying it with the jubilee year he was indicating the form that this fulfillment would take, namely freedom and prosperity for all.

Jeremiah: A New Covenant (Book of Jeremiah)

Jeremiah (circa seventh century) ministered in the southern kingdom of Judah toward the end of the reign of King Josiah (640–609 B.C.E.) until the Babylonian captivity (587 B.C.E.), and so he knew the efforts toward reform as well as the failures that they endured. While Isaiah seems to have welcomed his call to prophesy with enthusiasm ("Here I am; send me!" Isa 6:8), Jeremiah has been called "the reluctant prophet" ("Ah, Lord GOD! Truly I do not know how to speak, for I am only a boy!" Jer 1:6). The task that was set before him was not an easy one. He was appointed "to pluck up and to pull down" and "to destroy and to overthrow" and only then "to build and to plant" (Jer 1:10). This was an onerous assignment for one who did not want the job in the first place.

The prophet might have been heartened by the reform program of King Josiah, but with his death, Jeremiah lost confidence in the possibility of any long-lasting change of heart. The people were too entrenched in their bad habits. Furthermore, they believed that because they were living under the rule of a Davidic king, they had God's promise that this peaceful arrangement would never change. Finally, they had the Temple in their midst. Surely the God who had preserved Jerusalem from the onslaughts of King Sennacherib during the time of King Hezekiah would make sure that it was safe from the Babylonians. Besides following a derelict style of life, the people entertained false hope. In the face of this, Jeremiah's commission was daunting.

There is a wonderful story that illustrates the complexity of the situation in which he found himself. Obedient to the word of God that directed him, Jeremiah presented himself to King Zedekiah with a wooden yoke on his shoulders, prophesying that Judah would indeed bear the yoke of exile in Babylon. Another prophet named Hananiah took the yoke from the neck of Jeremiah and broke it, proclaiming that God had broken the yoke of the king of Babylon. What was Jeremiah to think, and to which prophet should the king and the people listen? Sometime later, Jeremiah received another message from God. He returned to the king, this time wearing a yoke of iron. Within the year, the prophet Hananiah was dead and, not long after this, the word of the LORD spoken by Jeremiah came to pass. Jerusalem fell to the Babylonians, and many of the leading people were taken off into exile.

Although the bulk of Jeremiah's message was one of warning and doom, there are also many moving passages that speak of God's love and compassion. It is in these that we hear God saying to a sinful people: "I have loved you with an everlasting love" (Jer 31:3); "I will satisfy the weary, / and all who are faint I will replenish" (Jer 31:25). It is in Jeremiah that we read of the new covenant, the one that is written on the hearts of the people, the covenant that once again assures them that "I will be their God, and they shall be my people"

(Jer 31:31–34). This covenant promises to be different from the one they had transgressed by their sins. This guarantees something new, and it will be enacted "in the days that are coming," an expression that came to mean the end-time of fulfillment. Jesus, too, spoke of the new covenant when he told his followers that the "cup that is poured out for you is the new covenant for you in my blood" (Luke 22:20). Out of the desperation of exile, Jeremiah announced a coming time of fulfillment. As he faced his own moment of desperation, Jesus announced that that time had come.

Ezekiel: Symbolic Visions (Book of Ezekiel)

Of all of the mysterious visions reported in the Scriptures, those of the prophet Ezekiel (circa late sixth century) are the most unusual. The book begins with a description of his inaugural vision. Out of a windstorm came a flashing fire and, in the middle of the fire, was something like four living creatures of human form. Each creature had four faces, that of a human, on the right was that of a lion, on the left was that of an ox, and the face of an eagle was in the back. They each had four wings, straight legs, and soles like that of a calf's foot. Two of their wings touched the wing of another creature, and the other two covered their bodies. With great speed they moved forward. Next the prophet saw four wheels along side of each creature, a domelike covering over the four creatures, and the glory of God above all this (see Ezek 1:4–28). Like the burning bush out of which God had spoken to Moses, this heavenly chariot manifested the holiness of God.

The vision itself signaled the character of the prophet's ministry. The Book of Ezekiel is filled with descriptions of symbolic actions and pronouncements that call for explanation. What seems to be eccentric behavior on his part is really acted-out prophecy. He is told by God to sketch a map of the city of Jerusalem on a brick, construct siegeworks against it, and then lie for three hundred ninety days first on his left side and then on his right. This represented the punishment of the kingdoms of Israel and Judah respectively. He was also told to eat unclean bread to represent the desperation brought on by the famine that the people would have to face during and after the siege. Finally, he was instructed to shave his head and his beard, a practice that was forced upon prisoners and slaves. He was directed to divide the shaven hair into three parts and burn it. The three parts represented the burning of Jerusalem, death by the sword, and the humiliation of exile.

Ezekiel dutifully followed the directions that he received from God (see Ezek 4:1–4).

It was Ezekiel who saw what no Israelite thought would ever happen: the chariot throne returned and the glory of God left the Temple (see Ezek 10:1–22). If Jerusalem was the center of the life of the nation, then the Temple was the heart of that life. After all, it was the most sacred place on earth, the place where the glory of God dwelt in the midst of the chosen people. The entire cultic system had been developed in order to pay appropriate homage to God's glory as it was enshrined in the Temple. Years earlier the prophet Jeremiah had denounced the people for placing false hope in the Temple. He told them that just because the building had been in their midst and they had been observing certain cultic practices, they had no reason to believe that God would not punish them for their infidelity (see Jer 7:3–4). They had not heeded Jeremiah's warning and now suffered the consequences. Not only did the Temple not save them, but they would not be able to save the Temple.

As dismal as his message must have been, Ezekiel does announce future restoration. In two places the word of the LORD promises a form of transformation. The first incident occurs at the very moment when the glory of God leaves the Temple: "I will give them one heart and put a new spirit within them; I will remove the heart of stone from their flesh and give them a heart of flesh, so that they may follow my statutes and keep my ordinances and obey them. Then they shall be my people, and I will be their God" (Ezek 11:19–20). In a later oracle, this same passage is preceded by another promise: "I will sprinkle clean water upon you, and you shall be clean of all your uncleanness, and from all your idols I will cleanse you" (Ezek 36:25). It seems that God never leaves the people without a ray of hope, regardless of how slim it might be.

Questions for Reflection: *Many think that prophets are people who can look into the future. In reality, they are people who have insight into the morality of our actions in the present. Some have said that Gandhi and Martin Luther King, Jr. were modern prophets. Who would you add to this list, and why? Name some of the issues we face today that could use prophetic insight.*

Chapter 6

The Priests

The priests of ancient Israel basically had three major responsibilities: They were entrusted with the care of the sanctuary; they were mediums through whom God's will was manifested to the people; and they officiated at sacrifices. Their primary duties in the sanctuary included caring for the sacred objects that were preserved there. This became quite an important task when the ark of the covenant was housed at the major sanctuary and later in the Temple in Jerusalem. The priests delivered God's will in several ways. The first was a kind of oracular consultation. People would come to them at the sanctuary in search of a word from God. Using various devices such as the Urim and the Thummim, probably small stones carried in an apron-like pouch called the ephod, the priests asked God for a yes-or-no answer to the question posed by the petitioner. Besides this form of casting lots, priests would interpret the Law in certain ritual and ethical cases. Since the Hebrew word for law (tôrô) really means "instruction," the priests eventually took on the roles of teaching and preaching.

The third major responsibility of the priests was officiating at sacrifices, and their other two duties prepared them well for this one. Since they cared for the sacred objects, who better than they would be qualified to use these objects during sacrifices? Because they were the mediums of God's will, who better than they would know what God expected in sacrifice? In order to ensure that every detail of the sacrifice was performed with the greatest reverence and care, a very elaborate cultic system developed. It defined the limits of sacrifice: how, where, when, and by whom sacrifice was to be offered. It also set the necessary limits to the use of cultic objects and to the lives of those people who were involved in the cult. The Book of Leviticus, for example, is replete with cultic regulations, revealing a people who took the worship of their God quite seriously.

Priests were not divinely called, as were judges, prophets, and the first kings. Rather, as was the case with the kings after David, priests were born to their office. The priest-hood was generally a hereditary profession, although we do find that at times someone could be appointed to be priest for a person or a group of people (see Judg 18:4). The holiness that was required of the priest was not a moral value. Holiness meant that someone or something was fit for sacred use; it was not damaged in any way, but was intact; it could stand before the creator in the condition intended by the creator. Again, elaborate rituals were developed that sought to guarantee this kind of holiness or wholeness. These rituals are also found in the Book of Leviticus.

Israel's sacrificial system was quite complicated. The holocaust or burnt offering was the most solemn offering. In it the animal victim, which was unblemished, male, and of the appropriate age, was completely consumed by fire. Before this fiery offering took place, the animal's blood, which signi-fied its life, was sprinkled over the altar and over those involved in the sacrifice. There were thanksgiving offerings and peace offerings that included a meal in which the victim was shared with the priest and the one offering the sacrifice. Sin and guilt offerings were similar to this latter sacrifice, except for the fact that the person making the offering received nothing from the sacrifice; the priest and God shared it all. The animals sacrificed were sheep, goats, bulls, and turtledoves or pigeons. The Israelites also offered grains mixed with oil. Every feature of the sacrifice was an acknowledgment of God's total power and authority over life.

Throughout Israel's history, major places where God had been manifested to particular individuals were designated sanctuaries and altars were erected in those places. While there were probably many local sanctuaries, some of them took on meaning for more than the local inhabitants. The first sanctuary mentioned in the ancestral stories is Shechem, where Abram built an altar after experiencing the presence of God (see Gen 12:6–7). This sanctuary continued to enjoy great popularity. Jacob pitched his tent there after his return meeting with his brother Esau (see Gen 33:19). It was also the place where the covenant was renewed after Joshua led the former Egyptian slaves across the Jordan River into the land that God had promised their ancestors (see Josh 24:1–28). Finally, it was the site where the northern tribes met Solomon's son Rehoboam and rejected the rule of the southern Davidic kingdom (see 1 Kgs 12:1–16).

The sanctuary at Bethel, which means "house of God," is another important ancestral shrine. It was to Bethel that Abram moved when he left Shechem (see Gen 12:8). Jacob stopped at the same shrine on his way to Haran in search of a wife, and it was there that he saw the mysterious ladder connecting heaven and earth. As with Shechem,

Bethel retained its cultic importance during the time of the judges, because the ark of the covenant was kept there for some time (see Judg 20:18–28). With the division of the kingdom, in order to ensure that the people in the north would not go down to Jerusalem to worship God, two shrines were opened in the kingdom of Israel. They were at Dan, in the northern part of the kingdom, and at Bethel, which was close to the border with the southern kingdom of Judah (see 1 Kgs 12:29–33). It was at this sanctuary that Amos delivered the word of the LORD against the northern kingdom (see Amos 7:12–13). After the Exile, the descendants of Benjamin reclaimed it as part of their ancestral land (see Neh 11:31).

Two shrines gained great prominence during the period of the judges. The first was Gilgal and the second was Shiloh. The name Gilgal means "circle of stones." Like Shechem and Bethel before it, Gilgal was probably a Canaanite shrine before a notable member of the people of God appropriated it for the worship of the God of Israel. It was at Gilgal that the ark of the covenant was placed after the crossing of the Jordan River into the land of promise (see Josh 4:19). Both Hosea and Amos condemn the inappropriate worship that was carried on there (see Hos 4:15; Amos 4:4). The sanctuary at Shiloh has a similar history. It soon replaced Gilgal as the center of worship for the tribes (see Josh 18:1). The ark of the covenant was installed there, and it was to Shiloh that the boy Samuel was sent to live with Eli, the priest who was responsible for the care of the shrine. Shiloh itself was probably destroyed during the wars with the Philistines. Jeremiah the prophet used the fate of this once sacred place as a warning of what was going to happen to the sanctuary in Jerusalem.

Levi: The Priestly Tribe (Deuteronomy 33:8–11)

The Levites are depicted differently at various times in the history of Israel. For example, in ancestral narratives they appear as the descendants of the son of Jacob and Leah (see Gen 29:34). During the desert and tribal periods the Levites serve as priests. It was during that time of the monarchy—when the two priestly houses of Abiathar and Zadok appear to have enjoyed prominence—that the role of the Levites seems to have changed significantly. Their less than distinguished function is most obvious during the postexilic period, when they were secondary officials, aids to the more important priests. This discrepancy in their representation is probably due to the diverse origin of the traditions in which they are mentioned, as well as to the inevitable changes in the roles played by various religious personnel over the years.

The name of Levi does not appear in every listing of the twelve sons of Jacob. This is because the lists probably grew out of property allotments and Levi seems to have been a landless tribe. One tradition states that, because of its violence, the tribe was deprived of its own territory and was scattered throughout the land (see Gen 49:5–7). This is corroborated by the fact that Levites often appear as strangers, presumably homeless and unemployed, associated with the widows and orphans as recipients of the charity of other Israelites (see Deut 12:18–19). A second tradition claims that as priests, the Levites had sacred duties that prevented them from engaging in other occupations and, therefore, entitled them to be cared for by members of the other tribes (see Deut 33:8–11). Most likely there is some truth in both of these traditions. However, the actual facts of the matter have probably been lost to history.

In the earliest traditions the Levites are the priests. They are described as resisting the worship of the golden calf into which the Israelites fell while waiting for the return of Moses from his encounter with God on the mountain (see Exod 32:25–29). For this loyalty to God, they were granted the exclusive privilege of carrying the ark of the covenant (see Num 1:49–53). According to one genealogy, Moses and Aaron descended from Kohath, the son of Levi (see Exod 6:16–25). Thus the Aaronide priesthood was Levitical in origin. All genealogies are not identical and so this line cannot always be traced. According to the account of the entrance into the land, it was Levites who carried the ark of the covenant across the Jordan River into the land of promise (see Josh 3:3). While there are narratives that tell of non-priestly Levites living and working during the tribal period, neither the accounts nor the members of the tribe appear to be numerous during this period of time. What we do find are accounts about Levitical priests.

In monarchical traditions a distinction is made between the priests and the Levites, the former being responsible for sacred functions while the latter are secondary and less important ministers of the sanctuary. The complexity of the Davidic monarchy and the structures that he brought into his administration from the Jebusite city-state of Jerusalem may account for some of this. Levitical responsibilities varied after the Exile. In the postexilic community, their importance was drastically reduced. They were doorkeepers and instrumental musicians (see 1 Chr 23:4–5); they attended the priests, prepared the bread, and cared for the sanctuary (see 1 Chr 23:28–32); they led prayers and instructed the people (see Neh 8:7–9). The changes through which this group passed can be seen in the way their functions have been attributed to Moses, David, Solomon, Hezekiah, and Nehemiah.

Eli: The Priest of Shiloh (1 Samuel 1–4)

Eli appears to have been the principal priest at the sanctuary at Shiloh. He had two priest sons, Hophni and Phinehas, who did not faithfully carry out their priestly responsibilities and who were summarily punished by God. Eli, however, was devoted to God and was steadfast in carrying out his duties as priest. It was to Eli that Hannah brought her young son Samuel to serve the Lord at the sanctuary. It was to Eli that Samuel ran when he heard the voice of the LORD calling him, and it was Eli who instructed him what to say when it became clear that it was indeed God who was calling the boy.

Although Eli was a righteous man and a faithful priest, his sons brought dishonor to him. They both died in the battle against the Philistines that resulted in the Israelites losing possession of the ark of the covenant. Hearing of their deaths and of the capture of the ark, Eli fell backwards in grief, broke his neck, and died. He had been priest for forty years, but because his sons were dead, his immediate priestly family died with him. Most likely, Eli's importance to Israel was in his care and direction of Samuel, the boy who followed as priest in the footsteps of Eli, who was also a judge of Israel, and the one who anointed its first kings.

Aaron: The First of the Line (Exodus 4–40; Numbers 12)

Aaron was the elder brother of Moses and Miriam (see Exod 7:7). He accompanied Moses when he went to Pharaoh demanding the release of the Israelites from Babylon. In fact, God appointed Aaron the spokesperson because Moses claimed that his own lack of eloquence was enough to excuse him from confronting Pharaoh. It was Aaron's rod that turned into a snake when the Egyptian ruler demanded a miracle. The same staff turned the waters of Egypt into blood, and was used to strike the dust causing the plague of gnats appeared. At the command of God, Aaron accompanied his brother Moses as the other plagues struck the land of Egypt. His support of Moses is further exemplified in the story of the battle against the Amalekites, when he and Hur held up Moses' outstretched arms. Aaron and his four sons were chosen by God to be the first priestly house of Israel (see Exodus 28–29), and they were consecrated priests by Moses himself. At that time they assumed the responsibility for the worship of the people and for the care of the portable tabernacle, which they carried with them through the wilderness.

The Bible demonstrates a definite bias in favor of Aaron, yet he is the one who made the golden calf for the people when they grew impatient waiting for Moses, who was up on the mountain speaking with God (see Exodus 32). Despite the role that he played in this infidelity, Aaron was not punished. On another occasion, when he and his sister Miriam criticized their brother Moses for having married a Cushite woman, only Miriam was punished by being stricken with leprosy (see Numbers 12). Some interpreters think that this is because the Israelites could not imagine their first priest being ritually unclean, as that disease would have made him. They were in a situation where they desperately needed their priest and so, for the sake of the people, he was preserved from that affliction. Actually, the text does not provide us with any reliable explanation, and so we really cannot be sure why he was spared. What we do know is that two of Aaron's sons, Nadab and Abihu, sinned grievously and so were ultimately excluded from the priesthood. The line was continued through the other two sons, Eleazar and Ithamar.

Like Moses, Aaron died before the people entered the land of promise. Prior to his death, his priestly garments were given to his son Eleazar, indicating that the powers of the priestly office had been conferred upon this son. Aaron, not his brother Moses, will always be remembered as the one through whom the priesthood of Israel was established.

Zadok: David's Priest (2 Samuel 9—1 Kings 2)

The relationship between various kings and priests was one of intrigue and political expediency. During the last years of the reign of Saul, David seems to have been in a constant flight for his life, because Saul suspects and then confirms that the LORD has rejected him as king and has chosen David as his successor. He accepted help from whoever would offer it.

One of the places to which he turned was the shrine at Nob. The priests here provided him with provisions and gave him the sword of the giant Goliath, which had been preserved there. When Saul heard of this he was enraged and sent his men to punish those who had aided David. The king's men massacred the men, women, and children there—not even the animals were spared (see 1 Sam 22:1–23). One priest, Abiathar, whose father traced his line back to Eli, was able to escape. He joined David's company and, as a reward for his fidelity, David made him his priest. Abiathar served David for many years, but during David's last illness he aligned himself with David's son Adonijah rather than with Solomon. Although he spared Abiathar's life when he became king, Solomon deposed him from the office of priest and exiled him to his home in Anathoth. This shame was understood as the fulfillment of the prophecy foretelling the end of the line of the house of Eli (see 1 Sam 2:30–36).

The priest whose name appears along with that of Abiathar is *Zadok* (see 2 Sam 8:17). Zadok, whose name means "righteous," seems to have accompanied David throughout his reign. However, his presence is seen particularly during the struggles that David encountered with his sons (see 2 Samuel 9–1 Kings 2). Zadok joined the party of Solomon and was rewarded when that son succeeded his father to the throne. He not only became the major priest of the kingdom of Solomon but, according to the prophet Ezekiel, the postexilic priesthood was restricted to the Zadokites, the priestly line that he established (see Ezek 40:46). Until the time of Antiochus Epiphanes (cir. 167 B.C.E.), the office of high priest was occupied by a Zadokite priest. Their loss of this office and the installment of a non-Zadokite priest enraged members of a religious sect that eventually separated itself from the priestly leaders in Jerusalem and founded a community in the wilderness at Qumran, the community associated with the Dead Sea scrolls.

Zadok's own descent is disputed by scholars. Some believe that he was from the house of Eli, but biblical evidence challenges this. Others think that he served at Gibeon before David brought him to Jerusalem. Most believe that the lineage supplied for him is a fiction intended to legitimate his priesthood. He may well have been a Jebusite priest attached to the shrine at Jerusalem at the time of David's conquest of that city. According to this theory, he was a member of the personnel who merely transferred their allegiance to the victorious king and his God YHWH. Most recently, some scholars hold that he belonged to an Aaronide family, and that the tension between him and Abiathar represented the conflict between the Mushite priesthood that descended from Moses and the Aaronide family that had roots in Hebron.

Questions for Reflection: *All cultures have recognized the basic need of human beings to relate with the transcendent. Various forms of worship have developed out of this recognition. In light of this, explain what people mean when they say, "I am not religious, but I am spiritual." What do you think of this statement? What about formal religion nourishes your spirit? What does not?*

Chapter 7

The Wise Ones

Until recently, scholars have maintained that the overarching theme of the First Testament is what has come to be known as "salvation history," the activity of God in the lives of the people. The texts do clearly show that the Israelites believed that God had chosen them, guided them, revealed the Law to them, and rewarded and punished them according to their fidelity to that Law. In effect, God was perceived as the principal actor in the drama of their history.

However, new interest in the natural world and the laws that govern it have resulted in another way of understanding the writings of the Bible. Contemporary commentators are beginning to recognize the importance, perhaps even pre-dominance, of another point of view. This view suggests that the natural world is the basis of everything and that God can be known through the experiences of everyday life, experiences that do not necessarily contribute to the national story of Israel. This perspective, known as "wisdom," is more interested in the unfolding of life in general and the successful living of that life in particular. Since the Israelites maintained that their God was responsible for the world and everything within it, they believed that living in harmony with this world and with others was both the basis for and the consequence of their relationship with God.

These two quite different perspectives flow from the same fundamental conviction, namely, that God is involved both in nature and in human history and through this involvement is accessible to women and men. This means that human experience, whether within national events, the particular incidents in one's personal life, or one's experience of the natural world, is the locus of an encounter with God. It also means that the circumstances of life influence the way God is perceived.

The wisdom literature includes the books of Job, Proverbs, Ecclesiastes, the Song of Songs, The Wisdom of Solomon, and Sirach. Several psalms have also been classified as wisdom psalms (1; 37; 49; 73; 91; 112; 119; 127; 128;

133; 139.) The wisdom books deal with general questions of human welfare, human value, and human destiny, although the teachings relative to these humanistic concerns must be understood within the context of Israel's Yahwistic faith. The dominant presupposition of their message maintains that whatever benefits humankind is a good to be pursued and whatever is injurious should be avoided and condemned. Success or happiness is the criterion for evaluating any course of action and is also considered concrete evidence of the wisdom and the righteousness of the person who succeeds.

A sapiential wisdom tradition is not unique to Israel. All cultures, both ancient and modern, have treasuries of wisdom that have been gleaned from experience, have passed the test of time, and have been handed down through the generations. It is by means of such a tradition that individuals learn the values, mores, and patterns of behavior expected of members of the group. That Israel was not alone in its quest for wisdom may be seen from biblical references that show the esteem with which other nations held the wise person, especially the wise Israelite. Examples include Joseph in the court of Pharaoh (see Genesis 41) and Daniel in Babylon (see Daniel 5). Israel's search for wisdom was clearly part of a broad sapient movement that took root in the ancient Near Eastern world.

Several theological themes dominate the wisdom teaching. While·these themes are found in other places as well, they are of fundamental importance to the wisdom tradition. Chief among them are: retribution, the theory that good will be rewarded and evil will be punished; concern for origins (creation) and ends (death); and the incomprehensible in life. Since these are basic human questions, there is a universal and perennial dimension to them that explains the similarity of so much of Israel's wisdom to the wisdom of other societies, both ancient and contemporary.

Retribution: The principle that prudent or virtuous behavior will yield happiness and well-being, while reckless or immoral conduct will bring on adversity and grief is derived from their observation of occurrences in life. People learned from experience. They perceived certain patterns as working to their benefit and others as detrimental to their welfare. Often they expressed such insight in the form of proverbs, which are really descriptions of situations in life. Proverbs not only preserved life wisdom but also taught specific behaviors that would produce desired consequences. Eventually, such insights became the source of customs and even of laws.

Creation and death: In awe of the wonders of nature, the Israelites came to believe that their God was the great

Creator-God who was responsible for the world, its organization, and everything within it. They perceived this creator as not only the architect of the universe but also the one who sustains reality and safeguards its established order. They recognized that the splendor of creation could have come only from one who was both powerful and wise.

The wisdom books view death as the end of all of life's possibilities. At this time in its history, Israel had no clear teaching about life after death. For this reason the sages believed that this world and human history were the only stages on which the drama of life would unfold. If the curtain of death were lowered at a time and in a manner that prevented one from playing a role in the final scene, the conventional teaching of retribution would question the righteousness of that person. The untimely death of the righteous was a dilemma with which Israel struggled until it was influenced by Greek thought. That worldview, with its concept of immortality, provided new avenues for understanding traditional teaching about retribution and for broadening that teaching in new directions.

The incomprehensible in life: All of the theological themes already treated ultimately leave us standing in awe and wonder before mystery. Both the wisdom tradition of ancient Israel and our own experience persuade us that there is much in life that we cannot comprehend. Although the wisdom tradition taught that certain natural laws can be perceived and followed, it never taught that people would be in complete control of the world or of their lives in the world. Despite the assurance about consequences presumed by a strict theory of reward and punishment, the sages maintained that the coveted prize of wisdom is often unattainable. In fact, they insisted that the dimension of wisdom most desired—the wisdom that explains the universe and the inner workings of human life—is beyond human reach and resides with God alone.

Sage: Happy Is the One (Book of Proverbs)

Just who is the sage, the wise person? This question has vexed both the ancient Israelite and the modern searcher. Judging from one's circumstances in life, it would appear that those with the most are the wisest, for their prosperity could be considered proof of their insight. However, from a religious point of view, those who are faithful to their religious traditions are the really wise ones, regardless of whether their loyalty paid rich dividends in material measure.

Reflection on life and the observation of nature led the sages of Israel to conclude that there was some kind of order inherent in the world. They believed that if they could discern how this order operated and harmonized their lives with it, they would live peacefully and fruitfully. Failure to identify and conform to this order would result in frustration, misfortune, and misery. The primary function of the wisdom tradition seems to have been instruction in a style of living that would assure one of well-being and prosperity. Since its emphasis was on education and training, the literary forms found in this tradition function pedagogically. These forms include: proverbs that describe particular life situations; parables, riddles and questions that tease the mind and lead to new insights; and stories that have a moral to teach.

While it is true that proverbs preserve insights into life that have been gleaned from experience, each proverb depicts life only in a certain situation and under a specific set of circumstances. What is fitting in one context may be inappropriate in another. This explains why certain proverbs seem to contradict others (see Prov 10:19–21). Thus the wise person does not merely learn the teachings of the wisdom tradition and apply them to another setting; rather, the wise person is able to decide what is appropriate in each new situation.

Experience is both the originator of wisdom and the basis for criticism of its value. Wisdom is a dynamic reality. It takes seriously the tradition of the past but is absorbed with the needs of the present, needs that may at times move believers beyond their traditional understandings. Although we may have no comprehension of God's work from beginning to end (see Eccl 3:11), still we are instructed to "get wisdom" (Prov 4:5).

A careful examination of the literature of this tradition reveals several different yet related ways in which wisdom is understood and people were considered wise. First, the technical skill or dexterity of performance with which experts ply their trades or utilize their abilities is called "wisdom." These people are able to perform with such expertise only because they have studied the rules governing their respective professions or crafts, and have become accomplished in them (see 1 Kgs 7:13–24); Ezek 27:8–7). Wisdom is also attributed to those who demonstrate encyclopedic knowledge. Solomon, for example, is credited with a scope of knowledge and understanding unmatched in the world (see 1 Kgs 4:29–34; Eccl 47:12–16; Wis 7:7–22).

A second arena wherein one might develop wisdom is the field of human relations. There one learns to be perceptive, tactful, and shrewd. The wisdom books contain much instruction of this kind. In fact, some interpreters maintain that such teaching originated from and was used within professional schools established to train official diplomats or scribal leaders of the court (see Prov 25:1). Other commentators believe that this is too narrow an interpretation, insisting that wisdom teaching is really a kind of training for life that is necessary for all. Such training often takes place in the home and is provided by both the father and the mother (see Prov 1:8).

While both of these kinds of wisdom require the development of keen powers of observation in order to discover the inner workings of some aspect of life, the second kind of wisdom seems to be more highly valued than the first. Human behavior is less predictable than the raw materials used by an artisan, and those who are able to steer themselves through the depths and shoals of human relations truly deserve to be called wise.

Finally, it is in reverent obedience to God that real wisdom is attained. "The fear of the LORD is the beginning of wisdom" (Prov 9:10). Such fear, based on the recognition of the holiness of God, is not merely an attitude of mind. Rather, it is the motivation of all conduct, launching every venture, sustaining it, and bringing it to conclusion. This religious motivation transforms the entire search for wisdom into a religious enterprise. The fruit of fear of the LORD is a wisdom that opens the person to deeper reverence and, therefore, to broader wisdom. It is no wonder that well-being and prosperity were regarded as rewards for fidelity to God. Such thinking led the sages to the corresponding conclusion that misfortune and adversity were punishments for behavior that not only disregarded the natural order established by God but also disdained fear of the LORD itself.

Woman Wisdom: God's First-Born (Proverbs 8–9; Wisdom 6–10; Sirach 24)

The wisdom books contain traces of creation accounts (see Prov 8:22–31; Eccl 24:1–12). What sets these passages apart from other creation texts is the figure of wisdom, personified as a woman, found in this tradition. Although she herself comes from God, this mysterious woman clearly has an important role to play in creation. Some consider her simply the personification of a divine attribute; others regard her as a hypostatization. (A personification is an imaginative stylistic technique; a hypostatization treats what is normally a mere personal trait as if it were a person with a distinct existence.) In either case, one must ask: Why, if the creator is usually characterized as male, is the personification or hypostatization of wisdom female?

The figure of Woman Wisdom has been interpreted as an ancient deity. It is possible that the ancestors of Israel initially claimed to have many gods before they worshiped the LORD alone (see Gen 31:25–30). They could have believed in a goddess of wisdom on whom this figure is modeled. However, although primordial in origin and cosmic in influence, in Israelite literature this wisdom figure is clearly a creature of God. The representation does suggest that the kind of wisdom that human beings seek is somehow related not only to God but to the very first moments of creation.

Many of the traits that characterize Woman Wisdom are found in passages that describe either the wise teacher or the wisdom teaching itself. This is a very interesting point, because it presents a female figure as an example of this wise teacher or teaching. This is quite unusual for a society that is not only patriarchal in structure but androcentric (man-centered) in perspective. Woman Wisdom is frequently contrasted with a second woman, Folly (see Prov 9:13). Both of these women roam the streets of the city, inviting the naive to follow them. As is the case in actual life, it is frequently very difficult to distinguish Wisdom from Folly. These characterizations are probably nothing more than imaginative literary ways of distinguishing between the way of wisdom and the way of folly.

In one of the later wisdom books, Woman Wisdom is in search of a permanent resting place. "In whose inheritance should I abide?" (Sir 24:7). It is God who tells her to pitch her tent in Jacob, in Israel, in Zion, in Jerusalem (see Sir 24:8–11). This is the author's way of claiming that real wisdom is found in the religious traditions of Israel and not in the philosophical speculations and insights of Greece.

The figure of Woman Wisdom, the one who was with God at creation and who pitched her tent among a chosen people, influenced the way the early Christian writers described Jesus, who "was in the beginning with God" and who "made his dwelling among us" (John 1:2, 14).

Job: Too Wonderful for Me (Book of Job)

Even those who do not know much about the Bible are familiar with the figure of Job. He was "a blameless and upright man, who feared God and avoided evil" (Job 1:1). He was a very wealthy man with seven sons and three daughters, great flocks, and numerous servants. Unbeknownst to Job, God brags to Satan about Job's goodness and Satan challenges God to take away Job's family and possessions and then his health. According to Satan, Job will then blaspheme to God's face for, according to Satan, Job is righteous because God has preserved him from harm. Contrary to Satan's expectation, Job does not blaspheme. Instead, he praises God:

> Naked I came forth from my mother's womb,
>   And naked shall I return there;
> The LORD gave and the LORD has taken away;
>   Blessed be the name of the Lord (Job 1:21).

> Shall we receive the good at the hand of God and not receive the bad? (Job 2:10).

In the end, Job receives double what he originally lost.

Many see Job as a virtuous man whose patience was ultimately rewarded. Unfortunately, this is a very superficial reading of a much more complex book. Although Job is definitely virtuous, he is patient only in the first two chapters of a forty-two-chapter book. Job actually rails against God, not so much because of his loss but because he does not understand why he lost what he did. According to the theory of retribution, the good should be rewarded and only the wicked should be punished. Even God admitted that Job was blameless, upright, fearing God and avoiding evil (see Job 1:8; 2:3). Then why had he been struck down with such overwhelming loss and physical suffering? Since Job knew himself to be innocent, the only other possible explanation was that God was capricious, out of control, or actually unjust. Throughout his own speeches, Job accuses God of all of these things.

It is not that Job had an alternative way of understanding how life should work; he did not. Like the men who came to visit him, he understood reality from the point of view of reward and punishment. Although he did admit that life was mysterious, he still longed for justice. He had called for a court trial where God would be forced to account for Job's predicament (see 9:1–3; 16–18). Instead, his own knowledge and experience were put to the test. Question after question was put to him, each one challenging his understanding of some aspect of the universe or his control over it. All of the questions confronted Job with the limits of his own creaturehood. He was indeed rebuked by God but it was for the narrowness of his vision, not for any lack of integrity on his part. What was challenged was the scope of Job's experiential knowledge, not his uprightness.

Job's ability to comprehend life had become the standard by which he measured the providence of God. By means of God's questions about the universe, Job was brought to new insights as to the limits of human nature. The speeches of God to Job are considered some of the most beautiful nature poetry in ancient Near Eastern literature. Here Job was closely questioned about the primeval events and the marvels of the natural world. His ability to exercise dominion over wild beasts or fathom some of the unique characteristics of the animal realm was contested. He could only stand in awe of the magnificent governing structure within the universe, one that far exceeds human comprehension or control. He was brought to acknowledge the wisdom and the power of the creator. Here natural creation became the means of bringing Job to new insight.

The use of nature as a technique of instruction is a well-established practice in folkloric traditions, as we see in Aesop's tales and other places in the biblical tradition (see Prov 6:6–11). If Job could not even begin to imagine the many and diverse ways that God continues to sustain creation, how could he possibly fathom God's mysterious care in his own life? Through questions about nature, God led Job to concede that, just as there are mysteries here that are far beyond his comprehension, so there are mysteries in human life that he will never be able to grasp.

It is probably in Job that we find the most gripping realization of the immensity of life's incomprehensibility. Acknowledgment of this incomprehensibility brought Job to a new realization of the mystery of God. The upheaval of his own life and his firm conviction of his own innocence called into question the way he had perceived divine governance in his life in the days before misfortune engulfed him. Formerly, he had known of God through the testimony of the ancients as well as through the teaching of the sages (see Job 8:8; 15:18). Now his unexpected, breathtaking encounter with creation gave him experiential knowledge of his own, knowledge that assured him that God was indeed in charge even though he, Job, could not comprehend how God governs.

Although Job had never intended to snatch any divine privilege or status, he expected, even demanded, an insight into reality that was far beyond what he as a human creature had a right to expect. God's questioning sought to correct this by pointing out time and again that God was God and Job was not. The splendor of creation transcended Job's comprehension and he could only stand in awe and wonder. The purpose of his breathtaking experience was not meant to silence him, but to reassure him of divine control over the universe and to inspire him to confidence in this wondrous yet incomprehensible God. Job's questions may not have been answered as they had been asked, but his fears were dissipated and his trust in this mysterious God was restored.

The message of the Book of Job is both at the heart of the wisdom tradition of Israel and a challenge to it. It does not cancel the theory of retribution; we should expect the good to be rewarded and the evil punished, and we should appreciate and adhere to this. However, it does very strongly bring home the fact that there is much in life that is beyond our comprehension and control. This means that while we strive to live lives of integrity, there will be times when our only course is to trust that everything is in the hands of a loving God who is committed to what is best for us, even when this does not seem to be the case.

Ecclesiastes: Vanity of Vanities (Book of Ecclesiastes)

The Book of Ecclesiastes is a strange book. There is very little in it about God other than that God wants us to enjoy the simple things that life has to offer (see Eccl 2:24; 3:13, 22; 5:19; 8:15; 9:9). In addition to this, the one called "the Teacher" seems to do nothing but complain about what life has to offer, and this despite the acknowledged fact that he pursued every path to pleasure and was able to experience what he sought. One wonders how this can be considered the "word of God," and what lessons about life it has to offer.

The Teacher has been described as a skeptic, a cynic or, more positively, a pragmatist. Some judge his religious outlook hedonistic or pleasure seeking, while others think it is faithful to Israelite values. It is clear that he is disillusioned, yet he lacks the passion of a reformer and the vision of a mystic. This has led some critics to label him a frustrated man who is resigned to the injustice and meaninglessness of life, intent on making the most of any fleeting pleasures, all in the spirit of Epicureanism, a philosophical system that held that the highest good was pleasure. However, a careful reading of Ecclesiastes will show that he does not really despair of life, but he rejects unrealistic expectations regarding it. Ecclesiastes' real struggle is with the meaning of life, especially from the perspective of the theory of retribution. In this he is like Job. Three phrases characterize his judgment: "chase after the wind"; "nothing new under the sun"; and "all is vanity."

A chase after the wind (1:17): The Teacher set out to experience everything in life so that he might discover its meaning. Although he accomplished everything, he was left with the question: What use is it (see Eccl 2:2)? He consistently arrived at the same conclusion; there is no lasting gain, no tangible dividend. Everything is "a chase after the wind" (Eccl 1:17). According to the theory of retribution, his wisdom and wealth were concrete proof of his goodness and a guarantee of future prosperity. It is not life as such or the search for fulfillment in life that frustrates him, for he does advise people to enjoy what they can. What bothers him is the profitlessness of human striving. It is not fulfilling. Success and prosperity do not satisfy him.

The Teacher is also troubled with the inevitability of death and the sense of futility it often brings. Regardless of how one lives, death is the ultimate fate of all. Any advantage that one might have because of righteousness, wisdom, or wealth is only temporary and, therefore, empty. Death and the total relinquishment that it demands force the Teacher to question the value of any human accomplishment and to wonder if perhaps life itself is merely "a chase after the wind."

Nothing is new under the sun (1:9): We have already seen how the wisdom teachers appealed to the obvious order within the natural world to teach people to live in compliance with acceptable social custom. This technique is used to lead Job to acknowledge life's incomprehensibility. The Teacher points to the regularity in nature (see Eccl 1:2–11), but does so in order to highlight its monotony. The earth does not change; it seems constant. The sun rises and sets and rises again and sets again in the same manner day after day. Although the wind appears at times to be irregular, it follows certain paths that, upon observation, can be predicted. Even the sea,

Chapter 7

although constantly fed, is never full. The regularity detected in nature appears to be devoid of any progress. Nature shows us that there is nothing new under the sun.

Life itself follows the same kind of cycles. Momentous events do occur, but they seldom interfere with the fundamental rhythms of existence. Nature repeats itself and so does human history. Nothing seems to have lasting significance. In what may be the most familiar section of the entire book (see Eccl 3:1–9), the Teacher declares that each event of human life has its own appointed time. What is appropriate at one time or in one situation can be out of place when the circumstances change. There is a time to die as well as a time to be born; neither seems to have an advantage over the other. Still, we do not know the rules that govern these appointed times, and so we are helpless to control them—and may feel that we are at their mercy. We are reminded of St. Augustine's famous saying: "You have made us for yourself, O LORD, and our hearts are restless until they rest in you."

All is vanity! (3:19): This expression has come to characterize the entire book. The word *vanity* means "pointlessness" or "futility" and refers to something that may be real but has little or no lasting substance. The Teacher has accomplished everything he set out to do. Despite this he declares that "All is

132

vanity!" All of the energy he put into his projects was pointless; all of his toil was futile. One might expect him to advise against ever trying to be happy, but he does not. Quite the contrary! He urges people to enjoy what they have. He does not spurn the search for wisdom or the normal human striving for success and prosperity. Rather, he objects to making human accomplishment the primary or exclusive goal in life. He calls upon all to find pleasure in what they are doing and, if they are fortunate enough to become successful in the process, to see this as a gift from God that should be enjoyed. The real goal of life is living.

Questions for Reflection: *Who are the wise figures in your life to whom you would go for counsel? Give examples of people who appear to suffer innocently. How could you explain to them the reasons for their suffering? It has been said that young people today find life meaningless. Is this true? If so, why? If not, where do they find meaning?*

Chapter 8

Mysterious Figures

There are several individuals who move through the traditions of the First Testament who can only be described as "mysterious figures." They may have been actual historical persons, caricatures based on historical persons, or mythological representations of some aspect of the faith of Israel. Whatever their individual origins, each embodies profound theological meaning and some of the religious aspirations of Israel, and they have all been interpreted by early Christian authors as prefigurations of Christ.

To understand the meaning of these mysterious figures we must take into consideration the metaphorical character of biblical language. As God-oriented as our theology may be, it is still a human attempt to explain the ultimate mysteries of the world, the divine dimension of reality, and the relationship that creation has with the creator. No language can adequately express aspects of the realm of the transcendent. We can only speak of God and the things of God by analogy. Today we live in an empirical world of space and time where our belief is often explained in terms of philosophical abstractions and theological models and precepts. Contemporary theology, which is frequently a way of interpretation, tends to be systematic and apologetic. However, our biblical ancestors lived in a world that was fundamentally sacramental. Theirs was a world in which human existence, with its joys and sorrows, harvests and famines, births and deaths, was understood as connected to and filled with divine power. The religious language of the ancients was imaginative and paradoxical, attesting to their personal experiences of God and using whatever forms best communicated the revelatory character of those experiences.

Although at first it may be foreign to our way of thinking, the metaphorical character of the Bible continues to open us to possibilities of expression and insight that precise historical or philosophical explanation cannot provide. It generates impressions rather than propositions. It seeks to capture the power and emotion of the event of God and to draw us into an experience that transcends both the past and the present and opens us to the future. The mysterious figures of the First Testament can work for us in this way. If we can discover the religious meaning that they convey and the way the early Christians reinterpreted that meaning as they sought to understand and explain the mystery of Christ, these figures can open us to new insights as well.

Two very important theological concepts must be addressed before we consider these mysterious figures: eschatology and apocalyptic. *Eschatology* comes from the Greek word meaning "last things." It is the consideration of human destiny and the end of time. It is a view of life built on the conviction that life does indeed have a purpose and it unfolds within the context of divine providence. The ancient Israelites believed that, because God was faithful, all of the promises that God made would be fulfilled in due time, if only in some distant future. Throughout the centuries they trusted less and less in the ability of their own leaders to bring these promises to fruition, and more and more in the probability that God would somehow accomplish this. In other words, they believed that either God personally or someone empowered by God would intervene in their history and bring all things to a final conclusion. Their faith in God developed into eschatological hopes and expectations. Their trust in God's intervention developed into various forms of messianism.

Apocalyptic comes from the Greek word meaning "reveal." Closely associated with the idea of eschatology was the notion that the fate of the world had been determined at its creation. Some versions of this tradition even hold that the details of the future were written down and sealed, to be revealed when the appropriate time came. These secrets would be revealed only by God or someone appointed by God and, because they were secret, they would have to be interpreted. At the time determined by God, the seal would be broken and the secrets of the future, written down in the past, would be revealed in the present. Very often this revelation took place during a vision. Examples of this kind of thinking are found in both testaments of the Bible (see Dan 7:13–14; Rev 1:1–3).

The Messiah: The Anointed One

Messiah comes from the Hebrew word for "anointed." (The Greek word is *christos*, which explains the origin of the title added to the name of Jesus.) In the Jewish tradition kings, priests, and some prophets were anointed. As Israel began to look to the future for the one who would eventfully lead it to the fulfillment of God's designs, it placed these hopes upon one who was anointed. Because all of the leaders mentioned were anointed, it is understandable that each tradition would develop its own understanding of and expectations regarding the future "anointed one." As different as they may have been, however, all these traditions did have one thing in common: they expected a messiah who would come into this world of time and place. In other words, the coming of the messiah would be a historical event.

Royal messianism probably developed out of the tradition of the everlasting dynasty promised to David. During the postexilic period with its profound disappointment with the kings, these expectations seem to have receded into the background of their people's thinking. However, they emerged anew when the monarchy was reestablished after the Maccabean revolt against Greek domination, around 164 B.C.E. The strong influence of the priesthood at this time resulted in the development of a priestly or Aaronic messianic tradition along side the royal or Davidic one. The Dead Sea scrolls show that the community that produced them was waiting for both messiahs.

These two messianic figures were believed to be human beings designated by God to bring about the time of fulfillment. However, another tradition developed that conceived of the messiah as "one like a son of man, " who would come on the clouds and be given an other-worldly kingdom by God (see Dan 7:13–14). This figure is found in latter Jewish apocalyptic writings. The Jews do not seem to have thought of the messiah as one who would suffer and, therefore, they did not consider the suffering servant found in the pages of the prophet Isaiah to be a messianic figure. It was the Christian community that brought all of these traditions together in their attempt to understand Jesus as the fulfillment of all of the expectations of Israel.

Belief in a messiah tells us at least two things about the believers. First, they are people who acknowledge that they are limited human beings and not the sole architects of their own destiny. Second, despite the apparent hopelessness of their lives, they are people who trust that somehow God will come to their assistance. People with messianic expectations believe in a better future, one that is in the hands of God.

The Servant of the LORD: The Chosen One (Isaiah 42:1–7; 49:1–7; 50:4–9; 52:13–53:12)

There are four poems in Second or Deutero-Isaiah that speak of a mysterious servant of the LORD. Although these poems have many characteristics in common, each one is also quite distinctive. For example, it is God who speaks about the servant in the first poem, the servant who speaks in the second and third, while God and unidentified persons describe the servant in the fourth. The identity of the servant has remained a disputed question to our own time. Some suggest that it may be a prophet, perhaps even Isaiah or Jeremiah. Others suggest that it could be Cyrus, the Persian king who freed the exiled Israelites and allowed them to return to their own land. These designations are questionable since in the second poem the servant seems to be the nation Israel understood collectively. In any case, the religious message of the poems is much more important than the precise identity of the servant.

The servant is clearly beloved of God, God's "chosen one" (Isa 42:1), upon whom is conferred a ministry of justice to all people (see 42:1, 4; 49:1, 6), particularly to those who suffer (see 42:2–3). The servant will establish justice (see 42:4) and proclaim the word of God (see 50:4). Probably the feature that is most prominent is the suffering that the servant will have to endure. The third poem suggests that he experienced hardship, even failure, in his ministry (see 49:4). However, both the third poem (see 50:6) and the fourth describe physical mistreatment. The latter poem is all about the suffering of the servant. In it we read that he was not only grievously abused, but that he took on the suffering that should have been borne by others precisely so that they would be exonerated of their guilt. It is no wonder that this poem came to be understood as being exemplified uniquely in the sufferings of Jesus.

Rather than presume that the author(s) of the poems had Jesus in mind, we should understand the relationship between this Jewish tradition and its Christian reinterpretation in the reverse order. In other words, the Christians saw Jesus by looking back to the Isaian tradition. As the tradition of this mysterious servant developed in the Jewish faith, it took on eschatological (end-time) meaning: it gradually pointed to a chosen servant of God in the future rather than one in the past. Since the first poem indicates that the servant was endowed with the Spirit of the LORD, he was soon considered one who had been anointed by God, similar to the prophet described in another eschatological passage (see Isa 61:1). Since *anointed one* comes from the same Hebrew word as does the word *messiah*, the Jews considered the servant to be a messianic figure of the future who would somehow lead them to a fuller understanding of their covenant relationship with God.

There are several allusions to this tradition in various gospel narratives, particularly the accounts of the baptism of Jesus by John and Jesus' transfiguration on the mountain. There we read that the voice from heaven speaks some version of the words found in the first servant poem: "Here is my servant, whom I uphold, / my chosen, with whom I am well pleased" (Isa 42:1; cf. Matt 3:17; 17:5; Mark 1:11; 9:7; Luke 3:22; 9:35). Scholars generally interpret these gospel narratives as occasions in which the messianic nature of Jesus' ministry is revealed. In this way the theology associated with the passages from Isaiah is applied to Jesus. He becomes the fulfillment of the eschatological expectations associated with the servant-messiah.

The Son of Man: Coming on the Clouds (Dan 7:13–14)

The Book of Daniel seems to be telling the story of faithful Jews who, at the time of the Babylonian Exile, refused to turn their backs on their religious practices even if their refusal put their lives in jeopardy. Actually, the details of the story, although taken from this period in Jewish history, are veiled allusions to the events that were taking place during the time of the persecution launched by the Greek emperor Antiochus Epiphanes (168–164 B.C.E.). Understood in this way, the book evidently is written in a kind of secret code that only the Jews could understand. This kind of "underground" literature is quite common among people who have a desperate need to communicate with one another but must do so in a surreptitious manner.

In the book, the main character, Daniel, has several visions. In one of them he sees a mysterious figure, "one like a human being coming with the clouds of heaven" (Dan 7:13). As is so often the case, it is difficult to determine the identity of this figure. He is a heavenly being, because he comes on the clouds. However, he is not God, because he is presented before the Ancient One. Some think that, like the servant in the second poem, he represents all pious Jews. Others consider him some kind of angelic being. As with the servant of the LORD, the role he plays is probably much more important than his precise identity.

This mysterious figure is said to be *like* a son of man. This means that while he may be in human form, he is not really a human being. He is a symbol. But of what?

He receives "dominion, glory, and kingship" (7:14), a description that casts him in the role of ruler. While he is somehow associated with the messianic king, the fact that he is not a human being suggests that this king and the kingdom that he receives are not human or political realities. Contemplation about this mysterious figure would have encouraged the Jews who were suffering persecution. To him was given all power and authority. If they were faithful, like Daniel was, they too would be admitted into his dominion that will last forever.

Of all the titles that contained messianic meaning, the Gospels have Jesus refer to himself as Son of Man. This title used when he talks about his messianic mission (see Matt 13:37), when he predicts his passion and death (see Mark 9:31), when he speaks of his return in glory (see Luke 9:26). While it is certain that the early Christians eventually understood

Jesus as this mysterious heavenly being, many scholars maintain that Jesus himself actually used the title, thus interpreting his messianic ministry within the context of that particular tradition. Whatever the case may be, the title has become prominent in Christian theology.

Questions for Reflection: *Christian writers have applied the features of the Messiah, the Servant of the LORD, and the Son of Man to Jesus. Applied to Jesus, what do they mean? With which one are you most familiar?*

Chapter 9

The People Who Moved the Tradition Forward

There were many other people who played prominent roles in the story of Israel, people who do not fit easily into a category. There were reformers and rebels; singers and lovers; Israelites who lived in foreign lands and foreigners who came to live in Israel; and women who put themselves in jeopardy in order to save their people. Several of the books in which we find these people are written in literary forms that are unusual even within the collection of biblical writings. The Book of Psalms is composed of various kinds of prayers; the Song of Songs resembles ancient Near Eastern love poetry; Ruth,

Tobit, Judith, and Esther are short stories set in one historical period in order to encourage people in another.

The Rebuilders: Ezra and Nehemiah (Books of Ezra and Nehemiah)

Ezra the priest/scribe and Nehemiah the governor are considered the builders of the postexilic Jewish community in Palestine, although they do not seem to have been contemporaries. Despite the historical discrepancies in the books that carry their names, it is possible to sketch a relatively plausible picture of the times from the data found there. Ezra was an official representative of the Persian court that had established a foreign policy quite different from the one operative in previous administrations. Those in power now believed that it would be to Persia's advantage to allow captive peoples to return to their homelands and resume their own religious and cultural practices, as long as they were considered provinces of the Persian Empire.

Authorized with a letter from Artaxerxes the Persian king, Ezra and a large party of Israelites traveled back to Israel in 538 B.C.E. to reestablish the nation. There he assembled the community and read the Law to them. It should be noted that as he read the Law, the scribes who accompanied him explained it to the people (see Neh 8:1–9). It is not clear whether this means that the people did not understand the Hebrew language in which the Law was read or they needed the Law itself explained. Whatever the case may have been, the reading of the Law took at least two days. The event seems to have been a kind of covenant renewal ceremony, similar to the one held by Joshua when their ancestors crossed the Jordan River into the land of promise after having been released from Egyptian bondage (see Joshua 24).

Once the people had been resettled in the land, Ezra inaugurated a kind of reform, forbidding marriage with non-Israelites and requiring those men who had entered into such unions to divorce their wives (see Ezra 10:44). It is not uncommon to find such harsh injunctions when a people is trying to rid itself of foreign elements that they may have acquired, and to return to the purity of their own religious life. The Book of Ezra recounts such events.

Nehemiah is described as a butler in the court of the Persian king. To him was given a letter of recommendation authorizing him to rebuild the city of Jerusalem. Although many people had been deported to Babylon at the time of the Exile, many others remained in the land of Israel. When Nehemiah arrived in Jerusalem, he encountered a group of these latter people who were settled around Samaria. Because they were opposed to the mission with which Nehemiah had been entrusted, they did what they could to prevent the accomplishment of his task of reconstruction. Nehemiah organized the builders in a way that allowed both defense and construction, and eventually the walls of the city were completed.

Like Ezra, Nehemiah forbade marriages with non-Israelites. He persuaded the Jews to lend money interest-free to other Jews who were in financial straits. In order to ensure the success of the newly built cities, he required a percentage of the rural population to move to these cities. All of this shows that he wielded tremendous power in the reestablished nation. Most likely this power stemmed from the authority with which he had been endowed by the Persian king, whose delegate he was.

Whatever we think about the details of the ministries of Ezra and Nehemiah, we must admit that they were men totally committed to the rebuilding of a dispirited people. The people who returned from exile were, like their ancestors, occupying land that was inhabited by others and consequently some kind of arrangement of settlement had to be agreed upon. The monarchy had been crushed and there was a need to reorganize political structures in ways that would benefit the struggling nation. The religious system had been dismantled and so religious practices and celebrations had to be reestablished. The nation as a religious and political entity had to be refounded, and the onerous task fell to these men. The subsequent history reveals just how successful they were.

The Rebels: Maccabees (Books of the Maccabees)

At the death of Alexander the Great (336–323 B.C.E.), his kingdom was divided among some of his commanders. Egypt was given to the Ptolomies, and Syria was given to the Seleucids. When the Seleucid ruler Antiochus Epiphanes IV rose to power, the full-scale Hellenization (the imposition of Greek culture) of the Jews was initiated. This meant that the observance of the Jewish dietary laws was forbidden and worship of Greek deities was mandated. The religious identity and commitment of Israel were under siege. The Book of Daniel, although set in the time of the Babylonian Exile, was written at this time to encourage the Jewish population to remain steadfast in their dedication.

One recorded incident describes an event that resulted in bloody reprisals. When a Jew stepped forward to offer adulterous sacrifice, a man by the name of Mattathias, filled with zeal for God, sprang forward and killed him (see 1 Macc 1:15–26). This began a national religious revolt. It was named after one of the sons of Mattathias, Judas Maccabeus, which means "the hammer." The name suggests the violence with which the Israelites fought back. Jews from all over the land joined in this revolt, which was led by Judas and his two brothers, Jonathan and Simon. Because of the power of the Hellenists, the Jews could not fight openly and so they engaged in what today would be considered guerilla warfare.

Two stories found in the Books of Maccabees deserve mention. The first is the account of the rededication of the Temple in Jerusalem after it had been desecrated by Antiochus in 167 B.C.E. He had installed a pagan altar on the very site of the altar of holocausts. This is what is referred to as the Abomination of Desolation (see 1 Macc 1:54). Three years to the day, Judas purified the sanctuary, erected a new altar, and dedicated it. A decree was issued requiring the Jews to observe the anniversary of this event every year (see 2 Macc 10:5–8). This is the origin of the Jewish Feast of Dedication or Hanukkah, an eight-day festival noted for its lighting of lamps.

The second story recounts how a mother and her seven sons were arrested and tortured in order to force their repudiation of Jewish belief and religious custom (see 2 Macc 7:1–42). The mother was made to watch their sufferings, but in doing so she also witnessed their profound dedication to the law of God. At the end, she too was put to death. What makes this narrative memorable is not only the deep faith of the woman and her sons, but their belief in life after death (see 2 Macc 7: 9, 11, 14, 23). This belief is also found in the admonishment to offer sacrifice so that the sins of those slain in battle might be blotted out (see 2 Macc 12:38–46). Until this time, we do not find mention of such belief in the traditions of Israel. However, as has been explained in the section on the wisdom writings, contact with Greek philosophy gave Israel the categories of thought that enabled it to develop its thinking in that direction.

Although the time of the Maccabees was one of revolt and resistance, it was also one of inculturation. As faithful as the Jewish community may have been to its religious convictions, it did incorporate many Hellenistic characteristics into its system of thought. Among them is the idea of life after death. In this, Israel may have chosen the path of the development of the justice of God rather than the immortality of the soul, but the Greek worldview provided it with a context within which such development could occur.

The Singers: Psalmist (Book of Psalms)

Just as there is a tradition associating Moses with all of the laws and Solomon with the wisdom writings, so there is a tradition that David composed the psalms. This tradition may be traced to the fact that several psalms are associated with David. However, as is the case with the other biblical personages, this association may be less historically precise than intended to provide authority to the writings. The psalms themselves give evidence of having been composed in various situations at different times and probably by many different people.

The psalms show that their authors were people of deep faith, people who brought every human circumstance and emotion to their prayer. Within the psalms we find sentiments of praise, grief, fear, repentance, confidence, gratitude, and national loyalty. They show that the psalmists were totally committed to God, employed various images of God, had great respect for natural creation and, while they gloried in God's mighty acts in their past, they looked to the future for the fulfillment of God's promises.

Psalms can be classified according to three major categories: hymns, laments, and songs of thanksgiving. The hymns (e.g., Pss 8, 29, 104) are songs of praise of God. Although many of them appear to be the prayers of individuals, most of them seem to have been composed for use in the liturgies of Israel's major festivals. The hymn begins with a call to praise, which is followed by an account of the wondrous acts of God, deeds that cause us to stand in awe and praise. There are also hymns that praise the kingship of God (e.g., Pss 47, 93) and there are some called songs of Zion (e.g., Pss 46, 76), which extol Zion as God's holy mountain and Jerusalem as the city God chose to inhabit.

Nearly a third of the psalms in the Psalter are laments, which are also classified as laments of an individual (e.g., Pss 22, 86) or of the community (e.g., Pss 53, 83). Although not all laments follow a general pattern, most of them consist of an invocation similar to the hymnic introduction; the actual lamentation that describes the suffering endured by the one(s) praying; a plea for deliverance from this misfortune; some kind of praise of God, often an expression of confidence that God will come to the rescue of the community or the individual; and usually a vow to perform an act of worship in gratitude for God's intervention. Some laments also include an acknowledgment of guilt or an assertion of innocence.

Finally, there is frequently a curse hurled against the one(s) believed to be responsible for the intolerable situation that occasions the lament.

Thanksgiving psalms, whether communal (e.g., Pss 65, 124) or individual (e.g., Pss 30, 138) are rather difficult to classify, because expressions of confidence and gratitude are often found within laments as well. This has led many interpreters to list these psalms with either communal laments (e.g., Pss 44, 74) or individual laments (e.g., Pss 4, 86). There are some psalms, however, that might be considered explicit psalms of confidence, both communal (e.g., Pss 115, 129) and individual (e.g., Pss 11, 62). Psalms of thanksgiving, again both communal (e.g., Pss 65, 124) and individual (e.g., Pss 30, 138), also comprise a distinct category.

In addition to these three major categories, there are others types of psalms. Several of them pertain specifically and exclusively to the king (e.g., Pss 2, 110), and are often referred to as "messianic psalms." They take on new meaning in the Christian tradition when they are applied to Jesus the king *par excellence* and the one "anointed" by God. Other psalms are clearly different in content and style from those psalms that probably originated in and were used during liturgical celebrations. They are concerned with teaching about the problem of evil, the suffering of the righteous, and the justice of God (e.g., Pss 1, 119, 127), themes that are addressed by the wisdom writings. For this reason they are referred to as "wisdom psalms." There are psalms called Songs of Ascent, that quite obviously were used during a pilgrimage to or procession around Jerusalem and the Temple (e.g., Pss 15, 24). Others were composed after the style of prophetic speech (e.g., Pss 50, 82). Finally, a small number of psalms seem to defy classification.

For Jews and Christians alike, the psalms are much more than profoundly moving poetry. They are the voice of our respective religious faiths. First heard centuries ago in a land far removed from us, they have been on the lips of believers in every historical period since that time. It is not merely that we use the psalms to express our devotion; our religious consciousness has been profoundly shaped by them.

The Lovers: Love Strong as Death (Song of Songs)

No book of the Old Testament is more difficult to interpret than the Song of Songs. It has been both a fascination and something of a riddle. It is clearly a collection of love poems full of sensuous imagery that promotes no apparent theological or moral values, and it never even mentions God. It is no wonder that its acceptance into the canon of inspired writings was seriously questioned by many people.

Just who are these mysterious lovers? The woman in the Song of Songs is identified as a Shulammite, perhaps the feminine form of the name Solomon. Some translations refer to her as a girl or a maiden in order to portray her presumed unmarried state. However, the connotation of youthfulness carried by these nouns also suggests immaturity, a trait that conflicts with the book's depiction of the woman. Furthermore, she is quite independent of societal restraints, in contrast to women in a patriarchal society. While she may be rather young, this is a mature woman, not a naive girl.

Although the Song is a tribute to mutual love, most of the poems depict the amorous disposition of the woman. Her words open and close the Song and her voice is dominant throughout. She is the one who is love sick (see 2:5; 5:8), longing to follow her beloved (see 1:4). She takes the initiative, seeking him both in the privacy of her room (see 3:1; 5:6b) and in the public streets of the city (see 3:2; 5:7). She is neither slow to speak erotically about their union (see 1:2, 4, 13; 3:4) nor embarrassed by the titillating language that he uses to describe her body (see 4:5–6; 7:2–10a). It is clear that this woman is driven by love, not inhibited by social opinion or by some narrow sense of sexual propriety.

The woman's description of the charms of her lover and the pleasures of their lovemaking, although often symbolic, is quite provocative. Her beloved is comely and agile like a young stag, renowned for its sexual prowess. The beauty of his body is praised part by part, from his head to his thighs (see 5:10–15). She rhapsodizes about the impassioned delights they experience that intoxicate like wine, and about those that can be savored like one savors luscious fruits. She relates how various luxurious aromas enhance the ardor of their passion. Sensuous metaphors such as these not only evoke vivid images but can arouse desire as well. This woman is not intimidated by eroticism.

The words of the young man are either in answer to the woman's questions or in dialogue with her. His first words acclaim her as beautiful, the fairest among women. No other woman can compare with her; her beauty is unblemished. The jewelry that adorns her makes her resplendence rival the most ornate of Pharaoh's chariots. Her eyes have enraptured him, even though they are as gentle and innocent as doves. Every part of her body is beautiful (see 4:1–5; 6:5b–7; 7:2–10a), and her voice is sweet to the ear. He compares her to a garden that is fruitful yet inaccessible to all but him. This is a man who has been smitten by love. His interest in the woman is certainly erotic, but there is no indication that he desires her merely for his own pleasure. The desire described in these poems is mutual, seeking mutual fulfillment. The woman is not being used; she is being loved.

While the book certainly applauds the glories of love-making, more importantly, it celebrates the depth of the commitment shared by the woman and man. She maintains that their love possesses a force that can easily rival the power of death and Sheol, the place of death. In other words, no power from the netherworld and no treasure from this world can compare with the strength and the value of human love. In the Song of Songs, fearless and undivided love is the greatest experience of life.

The Stranger: Ruth (Book of Ruth)

The Book of Ruth is a novella that tells the story of a Moabite woman who was not born an Israelite, but who became an ancestress of the great King David. The story takes place at the time of the judges, when an Israelite man, his wife Naomi, and their two sons move east across the Jordan River to Moab. There the sons marry Moabite woman. When the father and his two sons die, their widows must decide what they will do. Naomi resolves to return to Israel, and one daughter-in-law stays behind in Moab. Ruth insists that she will stay with Naomi: "Where you go, I will go; where you lodge, I will lodge; your people shall be my people, and your God my God" (Ruth 1:16). And so the two widows return to Israel to begin new lives. According to Israelite custom, if a man died without leaving an heir, his brother had a responsibility to take the widow as wife and raise up an heir for the dead brother. In an attempt to see that this obligation is fulfilled, Naomi orchestrates the union of Ruth and Boaz, a male relative of her deceased husband. From this union is born Perez, an ancestor of David.

This book is not only an engaging novel, but it also reveals some very important information about the customs of ancient Israel. First, the levirate law (from *levir*, Latin for "brother") demonstrates the importance of descendants who will preserve the name of the man so that it not be lost to history nor the land be alienated from the clan holdings. All of this would be very meaningful in a patriarchal society such as was ancient Israel.

Second, and probably more important, is the attitude of Israel toward the other nations. It is interesting to trace this attitude through various books of the First Testament. It seems that when the nation has a strong self-identity, it is not threatened by people with different religious convictions and practices. This appears to have been the case while David was king. He brought whole peoples into his realm, but the nation was strong enough to assimilate them into Israelite life and thinking. However, at times of great crisis, when their theological understanding did not seem adequate to explain the realities of life, the people were inclined to take on thinking that did offer an explanation. Actually, there were probably always people in the community of both mindsets regardless of the circumstances within which the nation found itself.

The Book of Ruth, although set at the time of the judges, was probably written after the Exile, close to the time of Ezra and Nehemiah. It addresses the very issue that concerned these two reformers: marriage to foreign women. However, it offers a radically different point of view. It demonstrates that not only can a non-Israelite become a devoted adherent to Jewish religious traditions, but God can even bring about the salvation of the people through such a person. For the Jews, this salvation was accomplished through David; for the Christian, it was accomplished through Jesus, a descendant of David. In other words, human beings may discriminate against some people in favor of others, but God does not.

The Healer: Tobit (Book of Tobit)

A second novella, although probably originating during the Hellenistic period (after the Conquest of Alexander), is set in Assyria and tells the story of a devout Jewish family who, having been deported from Israel in the eighth century b.c.e., was living in Nineveh. Once wealthy and faithful in giving alms, the family experiences financial collapse. When the father of the family loses his sight, he sends his son Tobiah to a city in Media to collect a debt owed him. The book is about the exploits of the son as he sets out to procure this much-needed money. Unfamiliar with the region to which he goes, Tobiah enlists the assistance of a traveling companion who, unbeknownst to anyone, is the angel Raphael. It is because he faithfully followed the counsel of this guide that Tobiah is successful in every one of his ventures.

The first unusual occurrence takes place at the Tigris River, where the two travelers have camped for the night. A large fish jumps out of the water and attempts to swallow Tobiah's foot. Raphael instructs him to catch the fish and take out its gall, heart, and liver and save them for medicine to be used in the future. Upon entering the region of Media, they stay at the home of a relative. The only child of that family is a young woman named Sarah who had seven husbands, all of whom died on the wedding night before the marriage could be consummated. According to the levirate custom, Tobiah has the right and responsibility to marry her. Although he fears for his life, Tobiah follows the instructions of Raphael. Entering the bridal chamber, he places the liver and heart of the fish on embers of incense that are in the room. The demon responsible for the deaths is driven out by the smell, and the couple passes the night safe from its terror.

The money is recovered and Tobiah returns home with a new bride. Reunited with his parents, Tobiah once again follows the directions of Raphael. From the gall of the fish he makes a medicine that he places on the eyes of his blind father, and the older man is healed. When the family tries to compensate Raphael for his extraordinary guidance of Tobiah, the angel reveals his true identity and, before their very eyes, ascends to heaven.

While the novella is a fascinating story in itself, filled with intrigue and magic, it also demonstrates several elements of Jewish piety and faith. The underlying premise of the story is the providential care of God. Although both the innocent Tobit and Sarah suffer grievously, God intervenes and saves them. However, this only occurs because of the unquestioning faith of Tobiah in following the directions of Raphael, whose name means "God heals." The piety of the characters is also evident throughout the story. The opening scenes show Tobit burying the bodies of dead Israelites, even though such pious practice was forbidden by the Assyrians who had captured them. When severely stricken himself, Tobit turns to God for deliverance. The same is true about Sarah; in her distress, she too turns to God in prayer. Finally, at the conclusion of the story, after Raphael has revealed himself and the way God's providence has worked through him, Tobit composes a prayer of praise and thanksgiving.

The story also shows the importance of certain social customs. The importance of proper burial rites demonstrates the piety of Tobit, as does his practice of giving alms. The contours of the family unit are carefully drawn. This is clearly a patriarchal family with Tobit as the head and Tobiah as the submissive son. Tobiah marries within his clan and the levirate custom is observed, thus assuring that inheritance will remain within the broader family. Every detail of the story shows that even though difficult, it is possible to remain faithful to one's religious practices while being exiled in a foreign and hostile environment. This was certainly a lesson that Israelites living in a later diaspora had to learn.

The Seducer: Judith (Book of Judith)

The Book of Judith is another novella. The heroine of the story is a widow whose name, Judith, is the feminine form of "Judah." As the story unfolds, the armies of the Assyrian king Nebuchadnezzar are intent on punishing the vassal states that refused to assist them in their wars against the Medes. Israel was such a state. The Assyrian General Holofernes has cut off the water supply of Jerusalem. For more than a month, the people of Israel put up a courageous defense, but their resistance is spent and they are ready to surrender. Onto the stage steps the widow Judith.

Clothed in sackcloth with ashes sprinkled on her head, traditional symbols of mourning and penance, Judith turns to God in humble and desperate prayer. She then washes herself and clothes herself in finery and, with a maid, leaves the security of the city and sets out for the camp of the enemy. The wisdom with which she speaks and her extraordinary beauty capture the imagination of Holofernes, and he is caught in the trap that she sets. He allows her to leave the camp at night to bathe in a spring. On the fourth night of her stay with

Holofernes, he invites her to a banquet for which she dresses in her finest attire. Thinking that a night of sexual delight awaits him, he drinks too much. Alone with him in his tent, Judith takes advantage of his drunken stupor and, with his own sword, cuts off his head. When she and her maid leave the camp with his head in her bag, the soldiers think that they are merely going out to bathe as they had done the previous three nights. In this way, Judith saves her people.

Some have criticized this book because it depicts a woman using her sexual charms to get what she wants. However, many cultures have a type of folk hero known as the trickster. They are the ones who beat their opponents at their own game. They are usually the underdogs of society who, because of their vulnerable situations, cannot directly challenge their rivals. They must trick them, and they do so with great skill and success, demonstrating that they are far more clever than the other. It is true that Judith used her charms to mislead Holofernes, not unlike the behavior of Jael, who drove a tent pin through the temple of Sisera (see Judg 4:21). However, she did so for the sake of her people and not for any gain for herself alone. Judith is a symbol of the entire nation of Israel, a nation that was held captive by the Assyrian army. In the face of impossible odds, pious Israel first turns to God in prayer and penance and then uses whatever means are at hand to protect the nation. The story demonstrates the courage of the faithful, the power of prayer, and the superior wisdom of God's people.

The Queen: Esther (Book of Esther)

The Book of Esther is another story of religious fidelity in the face of persecution, political and sexual intrigue, and the reversal of fortunes of those who threaten the survival of the Jewish people. Set within the context of the Persian court, it probably originated during the Hellenistic period, as did most of the other biblical short stories.

There are several interlocking themes in this book. One is the way women are depicted. The Persian king delights in parading his wives before his courtiers in order to display their beauty, a practice that is demeaning to women. When Queen Vashti refuses to be treated in this fashion, she is punished with dismissal and, lest other wives treat their husbands in this way, a decree goes out to the entire kingdom requiring wives to honor their husbands. The king then sets out to find a replacement for Vashti. A kind of beauty contest is held and Esther is chosen. Members of the court do not know that she is Jewish, and Mordecai, her guardian, instructs her to keep her true identity secret.

For his part, Mordecai not only continues to follow his Jewish practices, but he publicly refuses to accord a certain kind of homage to Haman, a high-ranking official. Enraged at this slight, Haman devises a plot to dispose not only of Mordecai but of the entire Jewish population. Although previously she had conformed to the palace's protocol regarding the conduct of women, now Esther acts in a manner similar to that of Vashti. The first queen had refused to come when summoned by the king; Esther approaches the king without having been summoned. Both actions demonstrate audacious behavior. However, God changes the king's anger to gentleness, and he receives her warmly. Now Esther uses her position as queen to thwart Haman's plot and actually turn it on the man himself. She reveals her true identity as well as his treachery. He is hanged on the very scaffold that he had erected for Mordecai.

The king then issues a decree that authorizes the Jews in the realm to defend themselves to the death against anyone who might attack them and steal their goods as spoil. Mordecai decrees that this event of salvation of the Jewish people be celebrated every year. Because Haman had cast lots in order to determine the fate of the Jews, the feast would be called Purim, which means "lots." It is celebrated to this day as a memorial of the saving power of God working.

This tale shows again the superior wisdom of the Jews in the face of their more powerful enemies. Like Judith, Esther used the weakness of her adversary to accomplish the salvation of her people. Although she was assimilated into the Persian court, she did not renounce her religious customs. When the fate of her people was at risk, she put aside her royal clothing, donned sackcloth and sprinkled her head with ashes, afflicted her body severely, and prayed for the deliverance of her people. It was only after she was armed with the confidence gained through such religious behavior that, uninvited, she dared to approach the king. Like Tobit, Esther shows that it is possible to be faithful to the religious practices of Israel even when one is living fully within another culture.

Questions for Reflection: *The Psalms are considered both Israel's and the Church's book of prayer. Many psalm verses have become part of common lore. What are some of the best known psalms? Which psalms are particular favorites of yours? Why? The Bible contains many stories of people who, though relatively insignificant in themselves, did something that contributed to the entire community. Name comparable people in your acquaintance who have made valuable contributions to the broader society. What contribution would you like to make?*

Epilogue

Some might wonder what value this First Testament might have for Christians. After all, they have Jesus and the Christian tradition that depict him as the fulfillment of the expectations of ancient Israel. Throughout the Christian centuries, that question has been raised time and again. There have been those who in some form or other have questioned the inspired character of the earlier testament. Most notable among these is the second-century teacher Marcion, who insisted that the God we meet in the First Testament is not the same as the God of Jesus Christ. Holding this error, he taught that the writings of the First Testament should be rejected. Marcion and his followers were excommunicated for this false teaching.

Then what value does the First Testament hold for Christians? This question can be answered in various ways. First and foremost, despite their struggle to understand how the two testaments relate to each other, the earliest Christians were convinced that both were avenues of revelation for believers. Together they show how God works in the lives of people, speaking to them through their various cultural understandings, calling them to deeper insights and a broader worldview. Together they reveal characteristics of God. In

Israel's notion of covenant, we see a God who is dedicated to a people, who remains faithful despite their disloyalty, who is always willing to forgive and embrace again. In the laws found in the Bible, we see a God who does not make impossible or illogical demands on the people. In the prophetic tradition, we see a God characterized as an aggrieved husband (Hosea), a nursing mother (Isaiah), and a stronghold of safety. The First Testament provides us with a glimpse of the God whom Jesus called Father.

Although both testaments do speak of a promise-and-fulfillment relationship, it might be better to see the continuity that binds them together. Both testaments depict the saving grace of God at work in human history. They share the same view of human potential and human frailty. They both speak of divine love and the call to return that love. They both emphasize the importance of community and the obligations we have toward each other. For Christians, the First Testament opens up into the Second, and the Second Testament presumes knowledge of and investment in the First. Christians hold both of them sacred.

For Further Study

Birch, Bruce, W. Brueggemann, T. E. Fretheim, and D. L. Petersen. *A Theological Introduction to the Old Testament.* Nashville: Abingdon, 1999.

Browning, W. R. R. *Dictionary of the Bible.* New York: Oxford University Press, 1997.

Crenshaw, James L. *Old Testament Story and Faith: A Literary and Theological Introduction.* Peabody, MA: Hendrickson, 1986.

Dillard, Raymond B. and Tremper Longmann, III. *An Introduction to the Old Testament.* Grand Rapids: Zondervan, 1994.

Doorly, William J. *The Religion of Israel: A Short History.* Mahwah, NJ: Paulist Press, 1997.

Farmer, William, et. al. eds. *The International Bible Commentary: A Catholic and Ecumenical Commentary for the Twenty-First Century.* Collegeville, MN: The Liturgical Press, 1998.

Flanders, Henry Jackson, Jr., Robert Wilson Crapps, and David Anthony Smith. *People of the Covenant: An Introduction to the Hebrew Bible* (Fourth Edition). New York: Oxford University Press, 1996.

Matthews, Victor H. *Manners and Customs of the Bible.* Peabody, MA: Hendrickson, 1988.

_____ . *Old Testament Themes.* St. Louis: Chalice Press, 2000.

McDarby, Nancy. *The Collegeville Bible Handbook.* Collegeville, MN: The Liturgical Press, 1997.

McKenzie, Steven L. *Covenant.* St. Louis: Chalice Press, 2000.

Murphy, R. E., J. A. Fitzmyer, and R. E. Brown, eds. *The New Jerome Biblical Commentary.* Englewood Cliffs, NJ: Prentice-Hall, 1995.

Meeks, Wayne, ed. *The HarperCollins Study Bible.* New York: HarperCollins, 1993.

Ord, David Robert and Robert B. Coote. *Is the Bible True?* Maryknoll: Orbis, 1994.

Pixley, Jorge. *Biblical Israel: A People's History.* Minneapolis: Fortress Press, 1992.

Smith, Gary V. *The Prophets as Preachers: An Introduction to the Hebrew Prophets.* Nashville: Broadman & Holman, 1994.

Stuhlmueller, Carroll, ed. *The Collegeville Pastoral Dictionary of Biblical Theology.* Collegeville, MN: The Liturgical Press, 1996.

Witherup, Ronald D. *The Bible Companion: A Handbook for Beginners.* New York: Crossroad, 1998.

Index

SHEED & WARD

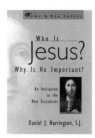
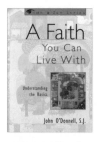
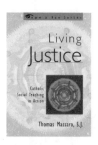